Good luck at Spring Creek! Daniel L. Shields

Fly Fishing Pennsylvania's
Spring Creek

Daniel L. Shields

Dedicated to the members of the Spring Creek Chapter of Trout Unlimited
With special thanks to Anthony "Tony" Gerace, who epitomizes the spirit and effort of Trout Unlimited

Acknowlegements:

The Good Lord, Creator of trout streams
My wife, Lynn. My children, Willy and Betsy
Flyfisher's Paradise staff: Steve Sywensky, Mark Antolosky, Doug Wennick, Scott McKee, Jim Kelly, Nelson Haines, Greg Hoover, and George Daniel
Edited by Robert Hass
Hatch consulting and editing from Greg Hoover
Photos from George Daniel, Nelson Haines and Greg Hoover, Front cover photo by Nelson Haines
Photographic and digitizing help from The Camera Shop staff
Map graphic from Chip Kogelmann
Fish and Boat Commission staff: Dick Snyder, Tom Wolfe, Marty Marcinko, Brian Burger, Bob Wilberding, John Arway, Sherry Lucas, Mark Hartle, Dave Bumann, and John Sinclair
Geologic and Hydrologic consulting from Mark Ralston
Legal and conservation consulting from Anthony Gerace
Interviews from Dan Alters, Roxanne Shiels, Mark Nale, Jason Wert, Ted Trostle, Karl Weber, and Jeff Spackman
Angling history from George Harvey, Joe and Gloria Humphreys
Advice and help from Ernie Erdeky and Jim McClure
Friendship and hospitality from Robert Hohn, James Houser, Paul Hutchison, George "The Gypsy" Lukas, and Jack Thorpe
Publishing help from the staff at Josten's

Hardcover ISBN: 0-9666882-2-8
Softbound ISBN: 0-9666882-1-X
Copyright© 2003 by Daniel L. Shields
Published by DLS Enterprises
PO Box 41
Lemont, PA 16851
814-237-2878

Product of The United States of America

Printed at Josten's, State College, PA

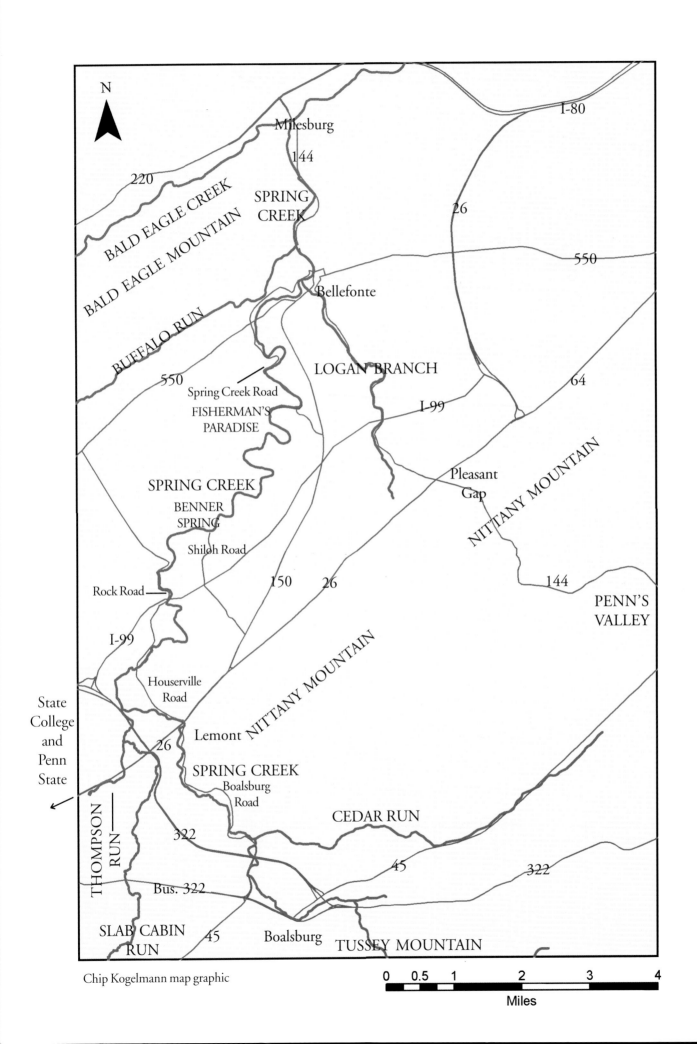

N

220

BALD EAGLE CREEK

Milesburg

144

BALD EAGLE MOUNTAIN

SPRING CREEK

I-80

26

550

BUFFALO RUN

Bellefonte

550

Spring Creek Road

LOGAN BRANCH

64

FISHERMAN'S PARADISE

I-99

SPRING CREEK

Pleasant Gap

BENNER SPRING

NITTANY MOUNTAIN

Shiloh Road

Rock Road

150

26

144

I-99

PENN'S VALLEY

Houserville Road

NITTANY MOUNTAIN

State College and Penn State

Lemont

26

SPRING CREEK

Boalsburg Road

CEDAR RUN

THOMPSON RUN

322

45

322

Bus. 322

SLAB CABIN RUN

45

Boalsburg

TUSSEY MOUNTAIN

Chip Kogelmann map graphic

0   0.5   1   2   3   4

Miles

Nelson Haines

Spring Creek graces the landscape it flows through.

Many trout streams are named Spring Creek, but none are more celebrated than the one in Pennsylvania's geographic center. First renowned as a stellar fishery, then as an example of environmental degradation, the stream is famous again as the Keystone State's best trout stream. Spring Creek educated thousands about fishing, and thousands more about conservation. Its story is hard to beat.

Spring Creek is a paradox. It is a quality trout fishery in an urban setting. No other stream in Pennsylvania has such abundant natural gifts, yet few are so plagued by man or as dependent on his beneficence for survival. Water volume declines while aquatic insect hatches resurge. Water unfit for human consumption grows more wild trout larger and faster, on a surface area basis, than all but our best tailwater and stillwater fisheries. Pollution renders trout unsafe to eat but also results in catch and release regulations that make a wonderful fishery.

Anglers' experiences at Spring Creek are likewise contradictory. Old anglers sadly recall opening day traffic jams and the glory of its now extinct Green Drake hatch. They also recall soapsuds piling up on odiferous riffles and how anglers deserted the stream after pesticides contaminated its trout. Today, rumors of good hatches and large trout draw eager flyrodders, who are quickly discouraged by crowds that mar the experience.

Another odd aspect of Spring Creek is the extent to which entities that harm the fishery also help protect it. A list of businesses and services in the watershed would reveal few that do not negatively impact the stream. But many of the same organizations provide help and leadership for conserving the fishery.

Spring Creek has earned a place in my heart through its contradictions. The highs and lows of my angling career occured there. The stream taught me more about fishing than any book, person, or piece of tackle. It has also thoroughly humbled me. I've caught more and larger trout there than anywhere else, and been soundly and very publicly skunked, too. My best angling friendships have cemented at the stream, often while witnessing outrageous angling ethical behavior. I thrill at improvements in the fishery, and despair over the watershed's continuing decline.

Fortunately, Spring Creek's good attributes still far outweigh the bad. If crowded, the fishing is often excellent. Traffic noise does not prevent trout from rising to sulfurs on magic spring evenings. Anglers, local residents, and conservationists enjoy and learn from the beauty that is the stream. Like Sylvester Stallone's mythical boxer, "Rocky," Spring Creek takes a tremendous beating, but it's a winner.

George Daniel

Wild brown trout are the reason for Spring Creek's popularity among anglers.

Natural History

God created few landscapes as pleasant as that which Spring Creek graces. The scenic topography is also the key to the stream's incredible productivity and resilience. In this watershed, like no other in Pennsylvania, precipitation drains so efficiently that two centuries' agricultural and urban development have not eradicated the fishery. Some of the water's flow is obvious, and surface channels tell a relatively recent tale of stream formation. Valley floors and ridge foundations hide another, ancient and more vital component of the fishery. Understanding how water flows through the drainage, and how man has altered the flow, helps anglers appreciate Spring Creek as a resource, fish it successfully, and conserve it.

Spring Creek's rocky foundations were laid down about 650 million years ago, during the Cambrian period. But it was not until the Ordovician Period, 150 million years later, that the most significant geologic addition to the future fishery materialized. At that time, plate tectonics had made central Pennsylvania the bed of a quiet, shallow sea whose fertile waters nurtured a myriad of now-extinct marine organisms. Dying, these primitive creatures left skeletons behind as calcium deposits, a phenomenon continued today by their tropical descendants. Over millions of years, the bony remains piled up into vast deposits thousands of feet thick.

About 450 million years ago, the restless earth shrugged its tectonic shoulders with a collision of the African and North American Plates. The cycle of calcium deposition ended in a mountain-building episode that raised the old sea bed and reared the Appalachian Mountains to colossal heights. During this time, erosion deposited sand and silt onto the old seabed. New deposition eventually rivaled the old, and their combined weight compacted the skeletal remains into carbonate rock, commonly known as limestone. The new layer of eroded material consolidated into sandstone or shale, depending on whether its origin was sand or silt.

Erosion gradually abraded the new peaks' raw edges into their softer present forms. The amount of material moved beggars description. Throughout much of Appalachia, *thousands* of feet of bedrock wore away. Enough rock to build every man-made structure ever built, including the Pyramids and the Great Wall of China, may have washed out of Spring Creek's watershed alone. In most of Appalachia the result was a crazy quilt of hills and hollows, but a different landscape emerged in central Pennsylvania.

Along the Appalachian Front, tectonic action, in combination with peculiarities in the deep crust, caused a singular washboard effect that tilted, folded, and faulted layers of rock strata. Where these movements exposed limestone beds, they washed away

Limestone springs keep Spring Creek ice-free in winter.

quicker than flanking sandstone patches. The result is a series of graceful ridges and valleys, startling in their regularity, that mirrors the ancient heavings of earth's crust. This region is Pennsylvania's Valley and Ridge Physiographic Province. In it, water repelled from the ridges' poorly permeable sandstone often disappears into sinks in the mountains' flanks, to reappear in bright springs in valley floors. The zone encompasses the natal valleys of the best natural trout streams in eastern North America. Penn's Creek, Fishing and Spruce Creeks, and the Little Juniata River are splendid streams, but Spring Creek's topography is unique.

Limestone is the most important element of Spring Creek's fishery. Where fractured by tectonic action and further eroded, it admits large quantities of water into the ground. In this drainage, massive amounts of water flow through and are stored in cool underground vaults and tunnels. Instead of rapidly escaping overland as in freestone terrain, water here takes its time to exit. The captured groundwater is slowly fed into the stream at constant, trout-friendly temperatures.

The cold water supply is critical to the fishery during drought. During the drought of 2001, water temperatures at the Fisherman's Paradise stretch of Spring Creek reached 76 degrees on hot July afternoons. Fortunately, numerous springs and seeps throughout the length of the stream minimized migration, and much of the stream offered decent sport

under conditions that decimated other fisheries. This is in sharp contrast to freestone streams in summer, when trout may desert miles of water to congregate at tributary mouths and in a few springholes. Unlike many freestoners, Spring Creek is a four season fishery throughout its length. Each month of the year offers some different angling opportunity.

Spring Creek's water is also fertile because dissolved limestone is an excellent building block for the food chain. Unlike sandstone and shale, which were formed from inorganic matter, limestone is formed from life itself and retains minerals beneficial to invertebrates. In limestone watersheds these nutrients are constantly transported via groundwater flows to their end users living in the streams. A practical fishing result is that while freshwater crustaceans such as sowbugs and shrimp are uncommon in freestone streams, they abound in Spring Creek and trout eat them. Flyrodders are well aware of the effectiveness of nymph fishing on limestone waters. The reason is simple: there is more aquatic life in limestone streams.

Spring Creek's limestone underlay is also an excellent buffer against acid precipitation. While freestone streams in the Alleghenies twenty miles west have pH factors as low as 4 after rain or snow runoff, Spring Creek runs a healthy 7.5 to 8.5, with alkalinity ranging from 100 to 200 (variations due to location and flow.)

Limestone creates scenic and interesting wa-

Daniel Shields

Spring Creek draws water from mountain trickles like Galbraith Gap Run...

tersheds. Spring Creek's drainage begins outside of Nittany Valley, on the shaded slopes of Tussey Mountain. That long ridge, Nittany, and Bald Eagle Mountains are the most obvious geographic features of the drainage. Their stately forms dominate the landscape and provide an inspiring backdrop for angling exploits. They are also excellent vantage points, and a hike to one of the summits rewards the eye.

From the tops of surrounding hills, Nittany Valley appears flatter than it actually is, as distance minimizes terrain fluctuations. The extent of contour irregularities are apparent when the observer is in the valley. Hummocky hills and depressions, big and small, are separated by gentle slopes and abrupt outcroppings. Geomorphologists term this type of terrain as karst. In it, so much water is coursing underground that surface undulations are as often caused by substrate erosion as surface wear.

Nittany Valley is classic karst topography. Sinkholes dimple the land, and there are swales and channels, some quite large, without a drop of running water in them. The best known dry channel in Spring Creek's drainage is Big Hollow; it marks the location of a former surface stream drawn underground by karst processes. The subterranean flows are known as aquifers, and, like surface streams, they have individual watersheds. Most people see aquifers at their "mouths," which are springs that occur where hidden flows and

the earth's surface intersect. A fascinating geologic side effect is that Spring Creek's 174-square mile groundwater drainage basin, unseen but not undetected, is larger than its visible surface watershed of 146 square miles. Groundwater under adjacent surface watersheds flows toward Spring Creek, opposite the direction of surface water in those places.

The relative lack of permanent stream channels is in sharp contrast to freestone country, where almost every low point evidences flowing water. Limestone terrain contains more water, but less obviously because the water is conducted into substrate and out of sight. One of the first travelers in the region, the Reverend Philip V. Fithian, noted the peculiarities of the locale: "One great inconvenience, however, attends the place, the want of water. Some few springs there are of good water and in plenty, but there ought to be many unfailing brooks."
Linn's History of Centre and Clinton Counties

What puzzled the good Reverend is a boon to the fishery. Spring flow is greater in karst terrain than freestone country, and surface flows fluctuate less radically. Limestone streams rise slowly after rain, and drop more gradually than freestone streams. As we shall see, however, Spring Creek is an unfortunate example of how man can alter the natural discharge of a limestone drainage.

Small surface waterways drain Nittany Valley's flanking ridges. With rare exception, they lose most if

...and from limestone springs such as Thompson's Spring.

not all of their flow, to sinkholes shortly before or after entering the valley floor. These minor streams are critical to Spring Creek's health, since they provide most groundwater base flow during drought. So efficiently is the little tributaries' water absorbed by the karst terrain that only in wet weather does surface runoff become a significant proportion of water leaving the drainage.

Karst topography radically affects the way Spring Creek grows. In Oak Hall, Houserville, and Bellefonte, the stream doubles in size from the influx of big springs and/or feeders that are themselves birthed from large springs. Significant springs also exist at the mouth of Big Hollow, Benner Spring, and Fisherman's Paradise. There are plenty of smaller springs and seeps, but their impact is not as dramatic as the big gushes.

Spring Creek is a great fishery because such a large volume of water emanates from its feeder aquifers. Some Pennsylvania limestoners, like those in the Cumberland Valley, have a greater proportion of their water originating from springs. Others, such as Penn's Creek and the Little Juniata River, are larger but more influenced by freestone feeders. Spring Creek is special because it has the largest proportion of cold limestone water of any stream of similar size in the Keystone State.

The original fishery also benefited from the Creator's landscaping. Earliest records indicate that the watershed was mostly forested. Indians complained that "further to the north (of the "head of the Juniata" [River

Valley]) there was nothing but spruce (hemlock) woods and the ground was covered with palm brush (mountain laurel). Not a single deer could be found or killed there." *Linn's History of Centre and Clinton Counties* Chestnut trees and other desirable hardwoods were also abundant in this part of Appalachia. In places the forest opened up into small prairies. Portions of the upper end of the watershed may have been in the "Great Plains," an area near Centre Hall notable for its lack of surface water. Rare native prairie plants still exist in Big Hollow.

Foliage acted in concert with geology to enhance the fishery. Ancient root networks kept erosion at a minimum. Precipitation sponged into a thick layer of humus, which slowly trickled it into the ground. Shade moderated summer's heat and minimized direct evaporation. Prior to man's development, the Spring Creek drainage was a wonder of natural water conservation.

Human and Pollution History

Millions of years developed Spring Creek's watershed to a peak of efficiency. Unfortunately, man laid a harmful veneer over this splendid foundation in a much shorter time. The new geology and human demand alters watershed function and the fishery.

Artifacts found in Spring Creek's drainage suggest Indians lived there for at least 10,000 years before European settlement. The sites most used were near Milesburg and Millbrook Marsh, where a jasper quarry close to Penn State's Beaver Stadium furnished tool stone.

Large Indian towns did not exist in the watershed. The closest major Indian community was at Great Island (Lock Haven), on the West Branch of the Susquehanna. This was typical of Indian settlement in eastern North America, which concentrated populations in prime real estate of large river bottoms. Remote locations like Nittany Valley were used if fertile, especially in summer, but were often abandoned in winter in favor of more protected valleys. Archaeological digs tell us that Spring Creek was used chiefly by small bands, most likely family groups.

A well-traveled path ran from Great Island up Bald Eagle Creek and entered Nittany Valley through Spring Creek's water gap downstream from Bellefonte. This was the Bald Eagle Creek Path, which paralleled Bald Eagle Mountain in Nittany Valley all the way to Tyrone, where it then reentered the Bald Eagle Valley. This trail ran two offshoots through Spring Creek's watershed. The Kishacoquillas Path roughly followed Logan Branch, passing through McBride's Gap near Rockview Penitentiary on its way to present-day Lewistown. The Standing Stone Path left the Bald Eagle Creek Path somewhere along Buffalo Run and crossed Nittany Valley to Pine Grove Mills, where it ascended Tussey Ridge and proceeded to Huntingdon. Another trail, the Penn's Creek Path, traversed the upper part of the drainage through Pine Grove Mills, Shingletown, and Boalsburg on a course approximated today by Route 45.

The most violent era of Pennsylvania history immediately preceded white settlement of Spring Creek's watershed. The Iroquois Confederacy was the chief military, and therefore political, power in Pennsylvania prior to the arrival of the English. So strong was the Confederacy that it exerted a commanding influence hundreds of miles from its council lodge at Onondaga.

The Susquehannock tribe, which controlled much of central Pennsylvania in the early 1600's, was an enemy of the Iroquois. Fur trade wars and European diseases so decimated the Susquehannocks that by 1700 they were nearly extinct. Their demise left a vacuum in central Pennsylvania that the Iroquois filled with Delaware, Shawanese, and Tuscarora Indians displaced by Europeans along the eastern seaboard. In 1754, many of the refugees were infuriated by the white interpretation of the Albany Purchase (1754) as including more land than the Indians had agreed to, including Spring Creek's watershed. As a result, The French and Indian War that began that year in what is now southwest Pennsylvania quickly spread to central Pennsylvania.

In 1755, an English army under General Edward Braddock attempted to take Fort Duquesne (Pittsburgh). It was ambushed in the woods near the fort and almost annihilated. After the disaster, the French and Indians pressed their advantage. In the fall of 1755, they assembled a force of 1,500 men at Great Island. Advanced war parties traveled through Spring Creek's drainage, using the Penn's Creek Path as an approach to destroy white settlements along Penn's Creek. A few unfortunate captives were driven out along the same path and may have been the first whites to behold Spring Creek. French and Indian failure to invade eastern Pennsylvania was a major strategic blunder. No force of comparable size, experience, and morale stood between them and Philadelphia.

Pennsylvania was forced to renegotiate the purchase of 1754. Not until 1758 was a treaty signed with the Indians that firmly the watershed inside Pennsylvania. A combination of fear and travel difficulties, however, kept settlers out of the region until 1769. Captain James Potter made an exploratory trip to the region in 1764 and was so impressed with what he saw that he settled a portion of Penn's Valley that included part of Spring Creek's drainage.

The most famous Indian to inhabit Spring Creek's watershed was Chief Logan, after whom Logan Branch is named. He camped at Blue Spring, the source of Logan Branch, in the late 1760s.

In 1769, Andrew Boggs built a cabin just outside the drainage, a few hundred yards from the mouth of Spring Creek. He would be the stream's closest white neighbor for several years. In 1773 James Potter brought settlers to Penn's Valley and soon farms appeared at the upper end of the watershed. Reverend Philip Fithian visited Boggs and Potter on a circuit, and his record provides a fascinating glimpse of frontier life and its natural setting.

"Mr. Andrew Boggs lives here, 25 miles from Esquire Fleming's. We dined on fish-suckers, chubs, and venison. It is a level, rich pleasant spot, with a broad creek running by the door. Many of the trees on this road are cut by the Indians into strange figures — Diamonds, dead heads, crowned heads, initial letters, full names, dates of years, and blazes.

Soon after we had dined, two Indian boys bolted in (They never knock or speak at the door) with seven large fish, one of which would weigh two pounds. In return, Mrs. Boggs gave them bread and a piece of our venison. Down they sat in the ashes before the fire, stirred up the coals, and laid on their flesh. When it was roasted they ate it. They eat in great mouthfuls and devour it with the greatest rapacity.

This house looks and smells like a shambles. Raw flesh and blood, fish and deer, flesh and blood in every part. Mangled, wasting flesh on every shelf. Hounds licking up the blood from the floor. An open-hearted landlady, naked Indians and children, ten hundred thousand flies. Oh, I fear there are as many fleas!"

On the banks of the creek is a large quantity of spruce pine, bark black and fine. It is a straight, tall tree. The leaves are thinner, longer and of a deeper green than other pine. It makes an excellent ingredient in table beer.

At ten I took my leave, crossed a gap of Muncy Ridge (Bald Eagle Ridge. ed.), and rode eighteen miles through wild barren woods, without any trace of inhabitation or road other than the blind, unfrequented path which I tracked at times with much difficulty. Two or three forsaken Indian camps indeed I saw on the creek bank (Spring Creek, Logan Branch, or Buffalo Run. ed.), and a little before sunset I arrived at Captain James Potter's at the head of Penn's Valley.

This ride I found very uncomfortable, my horse lame with but one shoe and a stony road. I lost my way in the gap of the mountains. More than ten miles of the way I must go and my poor horse without water. I let him feed in the woods, however, where there is plenty of good wild grass. I fed myself on huckleberries. In these woods are beautiful flowers and a great quantity and especially of a large, orange-colored lily, spotted with black spots. I saw here the first sloe, that grows on a small bush like the hazel, ripens in the winter and is now like a heart cherry. These woods have great plenty of wild cherry growing on low spray bushes, which are just now ripening." *Linn's History of Centre and Clinton Counties*

The American Revolution came to the watershed in July, 1778, when British efforts to incite Indians to attack Pennsylvania's frontier bore bloody fruit. Much of the fighting occurred farther east, where the Wyoming Valley Massacre claimed over 200 lives, but settlers near Spring Creek suffered, too. The following gruesome event occurred just inside the watershed, close to where the Kishacoquillas Path descended into Penn's Valley a few miles west of James Potter's Fort (Old Fort).

"Moore ... stopped at the cabin of Abraham Standford.... Upon entering the cabin he discovered that none of the family were in the house, but going around the cabin toward the spring he saw the body of Mrs. Standford, scalped and blood yet oozing from the wounds. At a few rods distance lay the bodies of two children. Life was hardly extinct in the body of Mrs. Standford." *Linn's History of Centre and Clinton Counties*

Incidents like this caused the "Great Runaway," during which settlers deserted the Pennsylvania frontier. Later in the war, American punitive actions destroyed Iroquois ability to wage offensive war. Indian wars plagued Pennsylvania until 1795, but little hostile activity occurred again in Spring Creek's drainage.

In 1796, Spring Creek was declared a public highway from Milesburg to the mouth of Logan Branch. But the most noteworthy use of the stream for trade was more an example of Bellefonte boosterism

Doug Kepler adds to his score during high water at Spring Creek.

than *bona fide* business. Bellefonte and Milesburg vied for the title of county seat, the award of which would bring commerce and prestige. Milesburg was favored because Bald Eagle Creek was more navigable and served a larger drainage, important considerations given the lack of roads. Some Bellefonte residents, however, loaded a flatboat with old furniture and towed the load with a mule team up Spring Creek during high water. They then informed the Pennsylvania Legislature that the first commerce barge of the year had reached Bellefonte. The ploy worked.

Bellefonte was named after its famous spring, called "belle fonte" by France's Duke of Talleyrand when he visited the town in 1795. The town still draws its water supply from the spring, one of the largest in the Keystone State.

Centre County's founding reflected population growth of the region. The first major push for settlement, and the first shock to the watershed's ecology, came after discovery of large iron deposits near the source of Buffalo Run. Combined with convenient local limestone deposits and forests, the ore at Scotia ensured that the region would become a major iron producer. Men who filed claims and built ironworks were a special breed known as ironmasters. Many were Revolutionary War veterans, hardy and determined — the type of men who build great nations.

Ironmasters imported whole communities into the watershed, thus ending frontier days.

The early iron industry used charcoal instead of coal for smelting ore. Large quantities of wood were required, and most of the watershed's old growth timber was cut down to fuel furnaces. Logging drives at the end of the 19th century completed the destruction of Spring Creek's old forest. The sawmills and tanneries the wood fed went the way of the iron furnaces, but left behind a denuded landscape. Today's forest has not expanded into the original acreage, but there are probably now more trees in the drainage than at any time during the last 150 years.

Centre County's iron industry flourished for a century, then ended after development of Minnesota's Iron Range. Philip Benner built the first forge in Centre County at Rock on Spring Creek, but natural landmark Benner Spring remains while the small town and dam that serviced the works are gone. Thompson Run was named after Moses Thompson, who owned Centre Furnace. Anglers can still see the remains of this furnace across the Benner Pike from the Duckpond.

The iron industry marked a turning point for the watershed's economy and fishery. Iron brought industrial growth to the region and made Nittany Valley thrive. Some enterprises spawned by iron outlasted the old furnaces and contributed to growth.

The first iron forge in Centre County was located near this limestone outcrop known as Rock.

Daniel Shields

McCoy's Dam is a reminder of Spring Creek's earlier use in local industry.

The ironmasters' stepchild, Penn State University, generated later development. As heavy manufacturing activity declined, Penn State, service, and light industries expanded. As pollution laws controlled point sources of pollution in the drainage, non-point pollution problems increased dramatically. The ironmasters played an important, if unintended, role.

In 1855, Pennsylvania approved the creation of a "Farmers' High School," and site criteria put Centre County in the running. Ironmasters made land and cash donations to secure the institution for Centre County, creating what would become today's biggest threat to the fishery: development in the upper Spring Creek basin centered at Penn State University.

Growth at the institution was slow at first, with only 69 students enrolled in the first classes in 1859. The "Farmers' High School" grew into a college and then, in 1953, a university offering a complete curriculum. Coincidentally, Penn State's impact on Spring Creek remained slight until the late 1950s.

Penn State's peaceful coexistence with Spring Creek changed radically on December 1, 1956. Years later, George Harvey recalled, "It happened ... when some cyanide was dumped down a drain at Penn State University. I heard about the spill at about eleven AM, went to the Penn State effluent discharge at Thompson Run, and walked downstream. There were dead trout everywhere. I had fished there a lot, and thought I knew how many trout were there, but I had no idea

there were that many. There were hundreds of them, floating belly up against the watercress. I ran into Dick Dalgren, the fish warden, and he had a bunch of dead trout from 18- to 24-inches on a rope. The spill killed fish as far downstream as Bellefonte and wiped out the food chain. Some of the hatches, like the sulphurs, came back, but the Grannom and Green Drake never did." *George Harvey: Memories, Patterns and Tactics* 150,000 trout were killed in Fish Commission hatcheries that drew water from Spring Creek. No estimate was made of the number killed in the stream. Spring Creek has never fully recovered.

As Penn State grew, so did State College. By the latter part of the 20th Century, Centre County's growth rate was one of the highest in Pennsylvania and attributable to Penn State. As you would expect, land near the University — the upper Spring Creek drainage — experienced the greatest influx of people and businesses. Development effects of dewatering, paving and consequent stormwater runoff, and sewage effluent are currently the biggest deleterious factors affecting Spring Creek, and threaten to dominate the fishery over natural influences. The problem grows worse as Penn State's expansion into non-educational venues paves more land.

Mercifully, many point sources of pollution in the drainage have at least been minimized. For instance, an investigation by the Fish Commission at Cerro Metal Products in 1952 found that the company ran as many as 33 outlets from its plants, which may have discharged liquids into Logan Branch and Spring Creek. The result: "Spring Creek was almost devoid of aquatic life and a greenish deposit existed on the bottom from its mouth to its confluence with Logan Branch, except for a short distance influenced by the Bellefonte Spring. ...Logan Branch was devoid of aquatic and fish life and a greenish deposit exists from its mouth upstream to the upper limits of the Titan Metal Manufacturing Co.'s (Cerro's previous name, Ed.) plants #s 1 and 4, a distance of 1.25 miles. Above these plants, Logan Branch supports abundant aquatic life." Pennsylvania Fish and Boat Commission

Cerro no longer discharges pollutants continuously, and effects of its former discharges have diminished. In 2000, however, an acid spill from one plant devastated lower Logan Branch. Food chain and trout were wiped out, but there is no evidence of permanent damage. On the plus side, Cerro has cooperated willingly with Pennsylvania's Department of Environmental Protection (DEP) and Fish and Boat Commission in correcting persistent discharges, improving habitat, and removing and/or capping decades-old soil and slag deposits.

Development increases the probability of point contamination through leaks in underground pipes and storage tanks. Leaks can go undetected for years, as the following example at Penn State shows. Contamination of soil and groundwater attributed to leaky fuel oil holding tanks was discovered during site preparation for a dorm complex. The housing that had used the fuel for heating had not used the oil since the late 1980s, but the leak was not publicized until June, 2002. Fortunately, contamination was slight and Penn State immediately began cleanup procedures, but the incident illustrates dangers posed by underground tanks and pipes. Should a pipe rupture near a sink, an aquifer can be contaminated in a few minutes but take years to recover.

The most notorious pollution in the watershed is from a chemical plant. In the mid-1950s, Nease Chemical Company applied for a permit to operate in College Township. Among other products, the company manufactured pesticides. Nease initially disposed of waste in state-approved "chem-fix lagoons" and on a leaching field behind the plant. More waste was stored in drums. The lagoon leaked, some of the drums leaked, and the leaching field worked too well: Chemicals from all three sources went into the ground. A year after start-up, aquatic life died in Thornton's Spring, whose aquifer includes the land on which the chemical plant stands.

An explosion at the plant in 1965 caused a large spill and fish kill. Karl Weber, now a partner of Richardson Chest Fly Box Company of Bellefonte, was a 10-year-old boy living in Houserville at the time. "A friend and I walked along the stream and saw loads of dead trout and suckers. Fish Commission personnel were throwing the dead fish onto the bank. The spill killed fish all through Houserville." A Fish Commission report indicates how bad it could have been, "By a miracle, 12 chemical holding tanks did not explode, or it would have been a complete wipeout of Spring Creek and possibly portions of Bald Eagle Creek." The community was lucky, too.

Between 1960 and 1971, Centre County Waterways Conservation Officer (WCO) Paul Antolosky fined Nease Chemical six different times for polluting Spring Creek. Fish kills resulted from "broken pipe lines," a "coincidental spill while transferring chemicals," "a tank trailer filled with butyl alcohol was knocked off its stand," and so on. In one of the worst spills, a pipe ran an estimated 15,000 gallons of noxious chemicals down a ditch and into the stream.

Groundwater testing at the plant produced ghastly results. "Groundwater at Nease was found to be contaminated with 22 different chemicals. The entire ecosystem was tainted with harmful hydrocarbons, which were being taken up the animal and plant life in and near the creek. Tainted fish were detected even in Sayers Dam, several miles downstream from the mouth of Spring Creek in the Bald Eagle Valley." *A Brief History of the Spring Creek Chapter of Trout Unlimited* Fearing liability, the Pennsylvania Fish Commission issued an advisory against eating fish from most of the stream the night before opening day of the 1977 trout season. Stocking was first discontinued downstream from the Benner Pike, then to Oak Hall when contaminated fish were found to have migrated upstream. Slab Cabin Run was later found to harbor contaminated fish that had migrated from Spring Creek, and a consumption advisory was issued for that stream as well. The issue caused a furor and, oddly, eventually resulted in better fishing in Spring Creek through imposition of catch and release.

The chemical company initially resisted cleanup procedures ordered by the Pennsylvania Department of Environmental Resources, but eventually implemented them. College Township now has the dubious distinction of having its own Superfund site. The chemical company now operates under the name of Rutgers Organics, and, to its credit, has not had any spills into Spring Creek for many years.

Until recently, one could smell the chemicals in Spring Creek downstream from Thornton's Spring. The reek is now gone because of the cleanup. Unfortunately, the same process that filters the groundwater also impacts Thornton's Spring's flow, creating yet

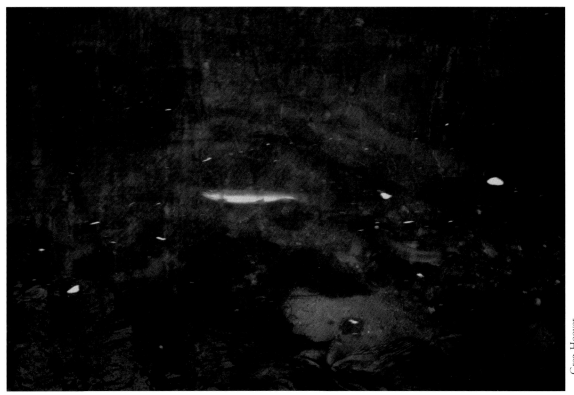

Greg Hoover

This photo of spawning trout shows exquisite timing. The female is cutting a redd. Two males fight over her.

another problem. Cleanup may continue until 2018, illustrating the difficulty of treating groundwater pollution. Treatment and time, however, are slowly working. In 2002, the consumption advisory for Spring Creek was lifted, but catch and release regulations for trout remain for sport purposes.

A new phase in the story began shortly before this book went to press, Rutgers Organics announced that it will idle the plant but continue cleanup procedures. If that happens, there will be one less threat to Spring Creek and continued improvement in surface and groundwater drainage from this particular site.

Many point sources of pollution at Penn State have also been largely remediated and/or minimized. For instance, the University's piled its coal supply a short distance from Thompson Run for many years. Runoff delivered acid-laden water into that stream, but natural buffering maintained a decent pH. The University treatment plant discharged sewage effluent into Thompson Run. The effluent was treated to pollution standards of the times, but fouled the water enough to make a fly line sticky.

The coal pile is gone. Better, a "living filter" project now delivers Penn State's sewage effluent to State Game Lands behind Toftrees development, away from any watershed surface stream. The liquid is sprayed onto land, where it percolates through the ground and is filtered en route to the water table. The project is a

tremendous boon to Spring Creek's water quality. After spraying began, weed growth diminished markedly in Thompson Run, lower Slab Cabin Run, and Spring Creek downstream from their influx.

Problems caused by limestone quarries in the drainage are harder to solve. A quarry near Pleasant Gap offers an example of the impact quarrying can have on groundwater flows in karst terrain. According to Robert Wilberding, Superintendent of the Pleasant Gap Fish Culture Station (fish hatchery), "The mine must pump groundwater to operate and intercepts much of the flow that feeds Blue Spring, the source of Logan Branch and water used by the hatchery." An agreement with the quarry resulted in water being piped to the hatchery. Unfortunately, in summer the water heats to as high as 75 degrees during its two-mile trip via an above-ground pipe, and the hatchery must pump supplemental groundwater to cool the water to below lethal temperatures. This is one of the factors that heats the upper part of Logan Branch to as high as 72 degrees in summer. The hatchery and the quarry are exploring ways of solving the problem.

Silt and gravel runoff from Hanson's Oak Hall quarry impact Spring Creek on and downstream from that quarry's property. The deposition fills in interstices between rocks, robbing trout and their food chain of habitat. Some formerly productive pools in this part of Spring Creek are so packed with gravel that only

Daniel Shields

This stretch of Spring Creek along Rock Road was formerly little better than an open sewer.

dredging can restore them.

The largest point sources of pollution, in terms of discharge volume, are municipal sewage treatment plants and the Fish & Boat Commission's fish hatcheries. Effluent impact on the fishery was worst in the 1960s and early 1970s. At that time, sewage plants and hatcheries had yet to upgrade treatment. My first fishing trips to Spring Creek were in autumn of 1974, and the stream's appearance and smell defied description. Suds piled up in eddies. Great masses of weeds choked the stream to such an extent that water was displaced and pools artificially deepened. Incredibly, goldfish had been stocked in the hope that they would eat the weeds, and their presence in pools where George Harvey caught native brook trout only forty years earlier was an affront. It was impossible to fish for long without catching a glop of elodea or filamentaceous algae. On these early jaunts, I often had to target and time casts to avoid undulating weed beds and floating weed mats.

Sewage severely degraded the fishery. Hatches other than midges did not exist between the University sewage plant's discharge point at Thompson Run and the confluence with Bald Eagle Creek — miles of water involving three formerly excellent trout streams. Thompson Run, lower Slab Cabin Run, and Spring Creek's main stem immediately downstream from its confluence with Slab Cabin all carried a visible load of suspended solids.

One of the worst discharges came from the Pennsylvania State Correctional Institute at Rockview. The prison's small plant discharged poorly treated effluent into a ditch that emptied into Spring Creek upstream from Fisherman's Paradise. The sight was bad, the stench worse. Ironically, trout flocked to the mouth of the ditch to feed on critters that thrived on the "bounty" and flowed into the stream with the discharge.

The University Area Joint Authority (UAJA) plant is the largest in the drainage. Prior to upgrade, it had a checkered discharge history. Fish and Boat Commission records document a spill in 1970 that dumped 130,000 gallons of sewage into Spring Creek. One month later, another spill from the same plant killed 1,100 fish in the stream. Only luck saved the Benner Spring hatchery, which at the time took water from Spring Creek a short distance downstream from UAJA's discharge. Only a year earlier, the Fish Commission had recommended that the authority end discharge from its plant because of environmental damage.

I killed a lot of trout in those days; they were a welcome addition to a student's menu. The first batch of fish I took from Spring Creek downstream from Houserville was also the last because they were caught at Rock in autumn. Time and place could not have been worse, because Rock is downstream from the UAJA and University plants, and by autumn even

14

stocked trout had all summer to absorb poorly treated sewage. Fishing buddy Jerry Trovato and I were proud of our catch, but everyone in the apartment complained of the smell when we fried them. We took one bite and threw the foul fish away.

Better days were coming. The UAJA plant has been extensively upgraded. Its personnel have garnered a reputation for professional skill, and the plant now discharges what a local engineer calls "the highest level of treatment in Pennsylvania, and possibly the United States." UAJA's efforts greatly enhanced the effects of the Penn State sewage plant's transition from in-stream discharge to the Living Filter. Spring Creek rebounded after these improvements.Hatches that existed only as relic populations became viable fishing events. Rockview Penitentiary now disposes its sewage through Bellefonte's new plant, but now prohibits fishing near the old ditch.

The drainage's largest water user and volume effluent source is the Fish & Boat Commission. Strong springs at Pleasant Gap, Fisherman's Paradise, and Benner Spring drew the (then) Pennsylvania Fish Commission to establish many of its fish hatcheries at those places. The hatcheries use over 15,000,000 gallons of water daily. In contrast, the largest sewage plant in the drainage, UAJA, currently treats less than six million gallons per day.

Unfortunately for Spring Creek's water quality, the hatcheries are extremely successful at raising fish. Millions of trout, shad, and various pike species are raised yearly. Uneaten food and treated fish sewage adds nutrients to the stream, and water temperatures change during the trip through raceways and settling ponds. Weed growth downstream from hatchery discharges is the most obvious sign of effluent overload.

The hatcheries are under increasing pressure to improve discharge quality. New effluent treatment systems were installed at Benner Spring in 1980 and Bellefonte (Fisherman's Paradise) in the early 1990s. Unfortunately, the upgrades did not prevent the hatcheries from being cited by DEP in 2002 as impairing biodiversity in Spring Creek downstream from their discharges. Total mass of the food chain was not hurt, as evidenced by hordes of sowbugs, but mayfly populations were depressed. The Fish & Boat Commission is actively engaged in plans for upgrading effluent treatment at all watershed hatcheries.

Sewage treatment has come a long way, but the watershed now faces an effluent emergency from the sheer volume of waste. If present trends continue, most of Spring Creek's water will be treated effluent in a couple of decades. Fortunately, Spring Creek's

Sowbug

overall status as a High Quality Coldwater Fishery sets high standards for discharge quality, including temperature restrictions. UAJA searched for alternatives to conventional disposal as it approached the limit of permissible discharge. Conservation measures, such as building codes requiring water-conserving devices help. The scale of regional development, however, render these efforts into mere delays before eventual sewage overload. Another initiative holds more promise.

"Beneficial Reuse" is the term that provides Spring Creek with hope for conservation and possible improvement. The plan calls for sewage, treated to drinking water quality at the UAJA plant, to be pumped back *up* the drainage and recycled by local industry or released into artificial wetlands constructed near Slab Cabin Run. The water will not be released at groundwater temperatures, but its journey through underground pipes should cool it below lethal levels. Better still, some plans call for the wetlands to drain into the ground in addition to overflowing into the stream.

As of this writing, discharge plans for the Slab Cabin drainage have not been fixed to artificial wetlands. There is hope in some quarters for an in-ground discharge. Such discharge would permit more groundwater recharge, and be better for the fishery. The least helpful discharge for the fishery would be a surge discharge directly into Slab Cabin Run.

Sewage recycling through Beneficial Reuse ameliorates several problems at once, at least in theory. Groundwater supplies will be less subject to depletion as less groundwater is pumped to industries using recycled water. Some water will be recycled more than once, compounding savings. Additionally, some recycled water will find its way back into the water table.

15

What will be the water savings? According to Jason Wert, engineer with Herbert, Rowland & Grubic, Inc. (the engineering firm designing the project), the watershed as a whole, and Slab Cabin Run's in particular, may end up a net gainer of water because recycled water represents extra precipitation. Says Jason, "As an angler, I would like to see more of this water reach Spring Creek in a way that helps the fishery beyond current discharge methods." In a best-case scenario, Spring Creek's volume could rebound instead of diminish, and Slab Cabin Run could become a viable trout stream again.

For Spring Creek, every silver lining has a cloud. Development interests may consider beneficial reuse as "The Solution" to water problems and claim implementation as a green light for unhindered growth. Execution will be fast for a project of this scale, but slow considering the need for relief from dewatering. The first industry hookups are targeted for 2005, with wetlands discharge planned for 2008. At least the initiative has developers, politicians, and environmentalists pushing for the same goal, if for different reasons. Let's hope the stream benefits.

Beneficial Reuse will not come too soon, because past and future benefits of cleanup and/or removal of point sources of pollution are being submerged by dewatering and stormwater runoff. This twin plague stresses the fishery and may eventually destroy it. In a nutshell, less water flows down Spring Creek, except when storm surges gush down the channel, carrying a wretched load of silt, contaminants, and, in summer, thermal pollution. Some parts of the drainage have already been ruined.

Dewatering devastates Slab Cabin Run, a major tributary. This stream's feeder aquifer provides much of the water used by the State College Water Authority's 60,000 customers. In dry years, the stream sinks through its bed in the vicinity of the Authority's wellfield along Branch Road. Trout as large as 19-inches are found dead in the channel's damp mud. George Harvey describes what we lost. "Slab Cabin Run used to have a great flow of water. After State College began to develop, however, the stream practically dried up. There was watercress in places along the stream — not much now. Before the town destroyed the stream, fishing in Slab Cabin was good, and I caught hundreds of trout there. I mostly fished in what is now the Centre Hills golf course. Back of the country club there was a big hole that was as wide as Branch Road, longer than the road is wide, and five feet deep. Fishing was also good above there, where Route 322 crosses the stream, and in what are now a trailer park and the Meyer Dairy Farm fields. My best catch on Slab Cabin, ten trout from 12- to 22-inches, came from that stretch."
George Harvey: Memories, Patterns and Tactics

Buffalo Run is another formerly excellent

stream impacted by dewatering. In severe drought, large sections of this stream disappear, leaving only a dusty bed as mute testimony to overuse of a resource.

The upper reaches of Spring Creek's main stem are also dewatered periodically. Water demands in the Boalsburg area are too great to sustain stream flow, and, like Slab Cabin Run, too many summers see fish kills. On one sad occasion, I counted sixty dead trout in one dry hole. When flow returns, trout migrate in only to repeat the dismal cycle.

By the time action can be taken, it is too late. In response to my queries about a local commercial nursery pumping irrigation water out of Spring Creek, WCO Brian Burger regretfully informed me, "A WCO working in the field can do little about water quantity abuses until the fish are flopping in the dry stream bed."

Farther down the drainage, flows at Benner Spring, which is monitored by the Fish & Boat Commission, fell from 5,500 gallons per minute (gpm) in 1950 to 4,200 gpm in 2000. Higher water temperatures reflect the lower stream flows. The highest reading George Harvey took at Fisherman's Paradise in the 1930s was 68 degrees. I recorded 75 degrees there during a hot spell in 1999, a drought year.

Dewatering's urgency as an issue is heightened by its impact on siltation. As flow decreases, so does Spring Creek's ability to keep itself clean. Silt builds up, and, as the streambed fills, water pushes to the side. The stream becomes wider and shallower as banks erode, causing more siltation. Destruction of riparian vegetation and dam building by landowners hasten the process. The vicious cycle is exacerbated by urban stormwater runoff.

"When I was a boy, some of the holes were deep enough to swim in. We used to swim in the Trestle Hole at Oak Hall and at a hole we called "Chin Deep" in Houserville. The dam upstream from Rock used to be six feet deep in places." *Joe Humphreys*

Stormwater runoff is bad and grows worse with each square foot of new pavement. Pools in Spring Creek's main stem immediately downstream from the Benner Pike (Route 26) are partially filled with road gravel. Smaller roadside ditches from Boalsburg to Milesburg also create piles of deposition. Thermal shock also occurs when rain falling on pavement heated to 120 degrees by summer's sun runs off far warmer than trout can tolerate.

Thompson Run is hardest hit because of its proximity to more pavement than any other stream in the drainage. The creek provided excellent sport, accidental spills aside, until the Benner Pike was enlarged in the 1960s. "When the Benner Pike was relocated, the stream was not taken into account. The old road went up around the

Penn State's Farm in Houserville. This beautiful stretch is badly impaired by stormwater runoff and attendant siltation.

old iron furnace. There was no reason they could not have kept it there. Instead, they rerouted Thompson Run into the Duckpond to make way for the new road. There were no environmental safeguards at that time. That road would not be constructed like that today." Joe Humphreys The project decimated Thompson Run's trout fishery. Much of the stream is now choked with road gravel.

I twice witnessed a stream of water, larger than most of Spring Creek's tributaries, flowing down State College's Calder Way during storms. Many town and University storm drains funnel into a channel up-gradient from the "Duckpond." Despite its picturesque name, the Duckpond is nothing more than a settling basin that drains into Thompson Run. Some good water from Thompson Run is diverted through the Duckpond, emerging polluted and, on hot days, warm.

The Spring Creek Chapter of Trout Unlimited, under Joe Humphreys' leadership, secured permission to reroute the spring around the Duckpond. In 1977, a dike was constructed in the Duckpond that kept good water segregated from bad. Results were impressive. After construction, summer water temperatures downstream from the Duckpond dropped radically. The effects were also felt in Spring Creek. This remains one of the most effective stream restoration projects that I have seen. "This was a real community project. John Miller at the University Physical Plant was a tremendous help. He realized that the spring should never have been pushed

into the Duckpond in the first place. We had incredible help from Glenn Hawbaker and his construction firm, as well as Centre Concrete, Herbert Imbt Construction, Sheesley Concrete, Claster's, and Neidigh's Quarry, all of which donated material and equipment. Trout Unlimited provided labor. After the dike was installed, gravel began to shine again at Fisherman's Paradise." *Joe Humphreys*

Thompson Run now holds some trout, but the Duckpond still causes problems. A pipe and channel are maintained between the spring run and the Duckpond, and good water is wasted in pond slime. "When I was a child, and until the Benner Pike was relocated, the Duckpond froze in winter because no springwater flowed through it. It was the most popular ice skating spot in the Centre Region until Penn State's ice rink was built. There was no history of permanent water flow through the Duckpond until the Benner Pike was relocated." Joe Humphreys

Runoff deposition in the Duckpond is staggering in magnitude. In 2002, the Duckpond was dredged. Jeff Spackman, project manager of the project for the University's Physical Plant, told me that he estimated between 9,000 and 10,000 cubic yards of deposition would be removed. In accordance with regulations governing disposal of sediments from such sites, the University tested for hazardous contaminants in the deposition. Those found were neutralized and disposed of properly.

Surface streams are not the only ones affected.

Benner Spring's aquifer is subject to stormwater runoff, and heavy rains turn its clear flow yellow with silt. The Fish & Boat Commission uses water from Benner Spring to raise fish at the Benner Spring hatchery. In 2001, stormwater runoff so clouded the spring that over 30,000 trout fingerlings died from suffocation.

Runoff also carries whatever chemicals are present on the surfaces it drains. Included in the brew are lawn, golf course and farm chemicals. Golf course and "small residential" runoff from the Elks Country Club were cited in the DEP's Aquatic Biological Investigation of 2001 as one of the causes of impaired aquatic life in Spring Creek upstream from Boalsburg.

A recent cause of runoff was the construction of I-99. This enormous project ripped through the heart of the watershed. During 2001, a drought and I-99 construction year, Spring Creek was frequently the murkiest stream in the area, a dubious distinction usually awarded to nearby Penn's Creek. I-99 construction, with attendant blasting, was the closest major disturbance to Spring Creek at the time, but tests to determine the source of siltation were inconclusive. In fact, all testing did was point out the difficulty of tracing and treating groundwater flows.

I-99 will also bring more traffic and the danger of accidental spills. Spring Creek is no stranger to this type of catastrophe. In 1972, a gasoline truck overflowed the tank at a gas station on the Benner Pike between Spring Creek and Dale Summit. Almost 2,000 gallons of gasoline flowed down the Benner Pike and clobbered Spring Creek from that point all the way to the Paradise. 25,000 trout died at the Benner Spring hatchery; nobody knows how many died in the stream. More recently, a fuel oil truck fell off a private bridge into Spring Creek at Rock Road. Luckily, the oil did not mix with the water and little damage was done.

Alien fish species, road runoff, dams and landscaping are all deleterious results of Fish & Boat Commission activities. Various members of the pike family are raised at the Benner Spring hatchery, and some escape. While brown trout are a welcome non-native species, the pikes are not. They range from Rock to Milesburg, and they do not eat mayflies. Commission road work upstream from the Paradise placed piles of dirt where it could wash into the stream. Commission dams at Rock and upstream from Fisherman's Paradise were originally constructed to feed stream water to the hatcheries. These dams block migration and divert water out of a fishery that needs all the water it can get.

Where hatchery landscaping needs have clashed with Spring Creek, the stream has lost. For instance, Commission personnel cut down trees between the Benner Spring hatchery fence and the stream. Reasons given were to prevent the trees from falling on the fence and to keep fallen leaves from clogging raceway screens. When I took issue with a hatchery superintendent about this, the official's response was that he had a million dollar facility to care for and had to give that priority. The official added that the bank had been sprayed with herbicide to inhibit new plant growth! Trees are growing again in the small riparian buffer left between stream and hatchery, but will the Commission cut them down? This problem has a minor impact on the fishery but should not escape scrutiny because the Fish & Boat Commission uses the phrase "Resource First" as a slogan.

The Commission is also good to Spring Creek. Pollution incidents in the watershed are quickly investigated, and the hatcheries are very concerned with groundwater. The Commission data bank has been useful in defending the stream, and its personnel often provide expert testimony in local water quality issues. Unfortunately, the Commission has less political clout than many of the entities that it tries to police. This must be frustrating to Commission personnel, the overwhelming number of whom are dedicated conservationists. After years of working with many of them on local issues, my impression is that their work is hindered by the bureaucratic nature of the Commission and occasionally by the Commissioners themselves.

An example of this occured in 2000, when the Commission balked at purchasing the property just downstream from Fisherman's Paradise. Formerly owned by Commissioner Oliver Deibler, who bought and posted it in the 1940s, the property was an opportunity for the Commission to right an old wrong — denial of public fishing access by one of its own. The Commission had the right of first refusal, and was aware that donations were available from interested anglers, businesses, and conservation groups. The decision not to purchase was not made by local Commission personnel, many of whom thought the Commission should buy the land.

A bright counterpoint to that failure was the Commission's purchase of the Levin property. An extensive tract of land on some of Spring Creek's best water, the property was posted against public access in the early 1990s. After much effort on the part of local conservation organizations, interested anglers and Commission staffers, the Commission bought the property and restored public access. Even this success story is marred, however, because the Commission had earlier passed up a chance to purchase an easement for

Daniel Shields

A descendant of Spring Creek's original salmonid, the brook trout.

much of the property at a lower price. The story points out the need for a more aggressive Commission policy of pursuing public fishing access.

Recent human impact on Spring Creek is a classic example of "good news, bad news." Water quality of the stream is probably better, with the exception of storm surges, than at any time in the last fifty years. But there is less water flowing over a silted bed. One would expect that the fishery was permanently destroyed by a myriad of pollutants delivered in terrible quality and quantity in both concentrated shots and steady discharge. Instead, the fishery rebounded as the worst of point pollutions were cleaned up or minimized. The stream's groundwater remains a counterbalance to pollution. When pollution decreases, the fishery has potential to improve quickly and substantially — if the water supply does not fail.

Pollution, however, alters the fishery. Pollution-imposed catch and release regulations enable trout to grow larger on a food chain supercharged by sewage and hatchery effluent. Pollution diminishes food chain diversity, but those organisms that do exist do so in great abundance. But sewage and hatchery effluent also cause aquatic weeds to run riot, and anglers curse the clinging green stuff and its constant fouling of leaders and flies. Winter water temperatures are artificially warmer due to sewage and supplemental hatchery pumping. This results in a longer growing season for trout. Pavement in the watershed helps the stream run off quicker than other nearby large limestone streams, assuming equal precipitation. Consequently, Spring Creek becomes fishable after heavy rains faster than, say, Penn's Creek or the Little Juniata River. Unfortunately, quick runoff is more an attribute of freestone streams than of a healthy limestoner.

The trout have changed, too. The watershed's original salmonid, the brook trout, populated the stream in profusion. Glimpses into the past are few, but tantalizing. "When I was a kid (in the 1930s) I ran into an old man below where the UAJA sewer plant is. He was sitting along the stream, and I sat down and talked to him. He said he had fished Spring Creek all his life. I asked him how the fishing was years ago. He said there was nothing but brook trout. He said there were brook trout of two pounds. They must have been 16-18-inch fish. He had probably fished the stream since the 1880s." *Joe Humphreys* A record left by Theodore Gordon reveals the numbers that a skilled angler could take in the 1870s. He also chronicled travel and accommodations of the era. "I ... took the railroad up to Bellefonte. ... Had a lovely room, 11 waiters, and excellent meals any time I wanted them. Stayed a week and never had a better time. One day I killed 40 trout but none over 1 lb." *The Complete Fly Fisherman The Notes and Letters of Theodore Gordon Edited by John McDonald* Brook trout persisted well into the 20th Century. "When I started fishing the stream in 1927, most of the trout were brookies. Some pools had hundreds of them." *George Harvey* George caught the biggest measured Spring Creek na-

19

tive that I have heard of, a 16-inch taken at Oak Hall. We will never know how big the largest grew.

Brook trout require clean cold water, and they dwindled as the stream warmed and became polluted. Brown trout imported from Europe also hastened the brookies' decline. In 1915, Theodore Gordon received a letter from a Bellefonte angler and relayed his message to Roy Steenrod. "The Brown trout have taken possession of the 2 streams that join just above and flow through the town. They get them up to 5 or 6 lb. now and then, but many fish of 16-18, 19 inches are killed." "He says that the show of big Brown trout on summer evenings makes your heart jump." *The Complete Fly Fisherman The Notes and Letters of Theodore Gordon* Brook trout provided a sport fishery in the main stem into the 1940s, but populations fell sharply thereafter. As late as 1990, I caught an occasional brookie in Lemont, but have heard of only three caught since then. Brook trout still exist in a couple of trickles that drain the surrounding mountains, and a few wild rainbows are present, but the fishery now relies on wild brown trout.

Robert Carline has studied Spring Creek and its trout to an extent that few others approach. "Perhaps the biggest professional surprise that Spring Creek has given me is the resilience of its wild brown trout population. If base flows hold up and water quality is maintained, there is no reason that the trout population couldn't rebound from catastrophe. Included in water quality must be water quantity as well as stormwater runoff and sedimentation reduction and mitigation. My studies show that sedimentation due to stormwater runoff and development are more harmful than other pollutants currently in Spring Creek. Studies of spawning habitat have been the most important ones that I made on Spring Creek, and I have found low embryo survival in some parts of Spring Creek due to sedimentation."

Geologically speaking, it took man the blink of an eye — 200 years — to alter Spring Creek's fishery right down to the fish themselves. The fishery will always hang by a thread due to its proximity with State College. It is possible that, by the time you read this, the stream will have experienced another disaster. If there is a good supply of groundwater available for the fishery's use, the stream will recover. Pollution can be cleaned up, and wild trout have demonstrated that they can dramatically repopulate the stream, especially with catch-and-release regulations. In other words, if we keep stream flow adequate and continue our work on pollution, the trout will take care of themselves if not overharvested.

Strong and growing public acceptance of the stream as a valuable state and community resource has also helped Spring Creek. A trout stream needs friends to survive, and Spring Creek's excellent fishing created them.

Angling History

"My outstanding memory of Spring Creek is the glory of the stream. The fishing and the atmosphere were amazing. You felt like you were part of something special to fish the stream." *Joe Humphreys*

Spring Creek had a good local reputation as early as 1872 or 1873. We are indebted to none other than Theodore Gordon, the pioneer of dry fly fishing in America, for an account of the stream at that time. Gordon fished Spring Creek on the recommendation of a Lock Haven hotel keeper, and mentioned the trip in an article published in a 1903 issue of *Forest and Stream* magazine. "Many years ago I was fishing a fine large limestone stream near Bellefonte, Pa., in company with a native of that town, who was a most expert angler and who cast in a particularly graceful manner. The scene of one afternoon's sport was a rather shallow mill dam constructed only a few years before; this dam was full of brook trout of about a quarter of a pound each and they were rising steadily all over the water. We cast and cast, and compared the flies in our respective books. Finally in the envelope in the pocket of his book my friend found a small straw-colored fly closely approximating the fly at which the trout were rising. He put it on and in half an hour or a little over, caught 42 trout. He had only one fly of the kind, so I was forced to play audience, nothing I could offer being tempting to the fish." *The Complete Fly Fisherman The Notes and Letters of Theodore Gordon*

Spring Creek's fishery made a lasting impression on Gordon. He tried to correspond with Bellefonte anglers for years, but was largely frustrated until 1915, the year of his death, when he wrote to Roy Steenrod. "I don't know whether I told you, that at last, yesterday I received a letter from a real angler at Bellefonte. I had been trying to get information, on and off, for ten years. Now I know why I got no replies. In such a large town there are a great number of local anglers who are jealous of strangers, and want to keep all foreign fishermen from taking their trout. . . I had such a delightful week at Bellefonte when I was 18 or 19 years old. Good hotel, everybody kind, and lots of very shy trout. I had one big day when I got 40 just before going home." *The Complete Fly Fisherman: The Notes and Letters of Theodore Gordon*

If local anglers did not publicize their bonanza, they made efforts to improve it. The first efforts to stock Spring Creek were made by Bellefonte residents. In its early days, the Pennsylvania Fish Commission shipped fry and fingerlings to interested anglers by rail. Records were kept of who received trout and where, but not which streams were stocked. Given transport difficulties of the day, we can be pretty sure that fish were not hauled very far from railroad depots. Commission records reveal that brook trout fingerlings were delivered into the watershed as early as 1883. Curiously, rainbow, or "California Trout" fingerlings ar-

Fisherman's Paradise on one of the first few days. George Harvey is fourth from right, instructing.

rived in the watershed in 1888, before the first recorded shipments of brown trout in 1894.

Through Gordon we have learned that fly fishing was as popular as bait fishing in Spring Creek as early as 1915. "All fish with fly. My informant sold 50 gross last spring, but for the town. For brown trout they use minnows on a special rig they make themselves." *The Complete Fly Fisherman: The Notes and Letters of Theodore Gordon*

Despite the stocking and good fishing, the reticence of locals and the stream's remote location crimped tourist traffic. George Harvey first fished the stream in 1927, and found little competition. "I saw only one other party of anglers during the first four years that I fished Spring Creek. They were from Altoona, and they filled a burlap sack so full of trout that it took two men to carry it. I also fished the Paradise area before the Fish Commission purchased the property. Fishing there was tremendous, and pressure nonexistent until the Paradise opened." *George Harvey* Even opening day of trout season was sparsely attended at Spring Creek. "Two of us had a mile of stream to ourselves on opening day in 1932, and the Commission had stocked it!" *George Harvey*

Spring Creek's obscurity ended abruptly in 1934. In 1933, the Pennsylvania Fish Commission purchased a property along the stream that included Forked Springs, which flowed 3,200 gpm. Construction of a hatchery began immediately, using the spring as water supply, and that portion of Spring Creek included in the property received extensive improvement.

The *Pennsylvania Angler* stated the object of the work, "It is the intention of the board to try out every type of stream improvement that can conceivably benefit this water, and study and record the results carefully."

Improvements included in-stream devices, stocking, and the first quality public fishing regulations in North America — perhaps the world. The project was called "Fisherman's Paradise." Success of "The Paradise," as it came to be called, was immediate and changed fly fishing forever.

Anglers at the Paradise were limited to five trips per year. They had to register and wear a button issued at the check-in booth. The project opened in May and closed in July, with no Sunday fishing permitted. Fishing began and ended with a klaxon at 8 AM and 8 PM. Fish caught outside the project had to be registered when the angler entered. Wading was prohibited, and the hatchery outflow was reserved for ladies only. Violators had tackle confiscated and their names and addresses publicly posted. But the most important regulations were those restricting anglers to artificial flies and a severely reduced creel limit: initially two trout over 10-inches. These restrictions, radical for the times, did not discourage attendance. By the end of the first two-month season, almost 3,000 anglers from 66 Pennsylvania counties, ten states and the District of Columbia had traveled to a remote district during a Depression year, voting for quality fish-

Daniel Shields

Fisherman's Paradise today. The fish hatchery is in the background.

ing with time, effort, and money.

The Paradise opened on May 25, 1934. The biggest trout caught that memorable day was taken by seven-year old Dave Shuey of Bellefonte, on a "cut rod and a heavy line." Angling authority Ed Hewitt was there as an observer, and the Fish Commission invited international fly casting champion, Art Neu, from New Jersey to give a demonstration. Hair Frog inventor Joe Messenger of West Virginia also assisted in the festivities. These men were first in a list of angling luminaries to attend the Paradise, which quickly attained a "must visit" status with flyrodders. But the man destined to be most famous in connection with the project and fly fishing was there before them.

"Fisherman's Paradise started in 1934, and I was there on the very first day as a Fish Commission employee." *George Harvey: Memories, Patterns and Tactics* George fished Spring Creek for several years before the Paradise was created, including the section that later became the project. In 1931, George enrolled at Penn State, where he established a reputation as an angler *par excellence*. George's college Dean, Ralph Watts, was an avid fisherman and so impressed with George's angling and fly tying skills that he persuaded his friend, Oliver Deibler, then Executive Director of the Fish Commission, to hire George to teach fly casting and tying at the Paradise. In that capacity, George taught thousands of anglers and was instrumental in developing aspects of modern fly fish-

ing ranging from fly patterns to casting instruction. His influence would be hard to overstate. An angling legend himself, Charlie Fox related George's prowess and how the Paradise acted as a fly fishing forum.

"In the day when a #18 fly was a Midge, 4X was a light-gut point, and a 7 1/2-foot rod a short one, we watched George combine these and, when the setup was right, hook trout after trout. ... In the last hour or two of the fishing day he would hook and land more fish than most of us caught fishing throughout the entire afternoon.

His testing ground was also the old Fisherman's Paradise, and what a convenient place for him it was. During the day George, in the capacity of a Fish Commission employee, gave individuals free fly-tying lessons or demonstrated fly tying to groups at the check-in booth. Here many of us got our start in fly tying. When fishing pepped up late in the afternoon, he fished. Thus he was offered an opportunity to experiment with patterns and styles, then he had the opportunity to test his wares. Usually he operated with one of his Horse-collar Midges and almost always it was before an unofficial gallery." *Rising Trout* by Charles Fox

The Paradise became incredibly popular. Fish Commission records for 1952 show over 44,000 anglers fishing the project, an average of 850 per day. The largest crowds were on opening day and Memorial Day, when as many as 1,500 eager anglers thronged the one-mile stretch. 12,400 stocked trout were added to the impressive population of wild trout, and 9,000 trout, averaging 16 2/3-inches, were killed. The biggest trout ever caught at the Paradise was a

22

Daniel Shields

The Paradise packs 'em in at sulfur time.

17-lb. brute taken in 1946 by Francis Partsch of Johnstown, PA.

The Paradise became a favorite of angling families. Gloria Humphreys recalls, "The Paradise was a beautiful place, like a park. In addition to the fishing, there was a nice stand where you could buy food or flies. You could tour the hatchery. There were picnic tables, but eating wasn't the main event. We were there for fishing, not food. My strongest impression of the Paradise is the air of excitement about the place. We were psyched up just to be there."

"The ladies' stream was fantastic. Something interesting happened every time I went there. The women were really wild and competitive. You'd hook a fish, and some woman fifty feet away would yell, 'You can't keep that one, it's foul hooked!' Some women would bring bait in and hide it where the wardens wouldn't search. Because you could keep one fish, and had to stop fishing if you did, there was always this mental game that you played. Should I keep a good one if I catch it in the morning, or should I hold out for a better one later?"

"One day I caught a 23 1/2-inch, 5 1/4-lb. brown trout at the women's stream. I kept that one! It was bigger than anything my husband Joe had caught at the Paradise up to then. I lorded it over him for some time."

Of course, Joe Humphreys has memories too! "My first shot at the Paradise was in 1936. My father took me down in his 1932 Willys. I went to the dam upstream from the footbridge. I could see lots of fish, and I flailed at them with a little streamer that dad had tied on for me. There wasn't a trout interested in my fly, but my first trip to the Paradise produced good memories. I remember how many people were there. I

remember them catching fish and the excitement that abounded along the stream. It was very contagious, especially for a boy."

"Here's how crowded the Paradise could get. One day in 1946, I pedaled a bicycle all the way down from State College. I got there late, and, by the time I got in, the banks were lined with people. I ran frantically up and down, trying to find a spot where I could elbow in. Finally, I crossed the footbridge and went up to the dam (now removed). Just below the dam was a big rock that slanted into the water. There was an old man standing on the rock, and I knew his stance was so uncomfortable that sooner or later he would move. As soon as he stepped off I jumped on."

"Something funny always happened. One time, two guys fishing across the stream from each other hung each other up. They got into a heated discussion, to put it mildly. One of them pulled the other fellow's line over to him and got it untangled. Then he stuck it in a log and walked away. At least they didn't hook each other. Someone got hooked every day."

"You couldn't fish at Paradise on Sunday, but you were allowed to look at the stream and feed the fish. People always threw bread off the bridges. Monday morning would see a crowd of fishermen lined up below those bridges, every one of them with a white deer hair bug — a bread fly — tied on. When the klaxon sounded, they would whack them in the water at the same time. People would get into fish, and it was one massive tangle. It was worth the trip to watch ten people try to play fish, some of them big, at the same time with the lines wrapped around each other."

"I worked at the Paradise hatchery when I was in school. The pay was low, but we got a fringe benefit when we cleared weeds out of the stream. We picked hundreds of lost flies off the

23

rocks and logs. The little island upstream from the footbridge was especially good pickin's. There were some logs jammed against it that were fly magnets."

"The Green Drake hatch at the Paradise was phenomenal. When that hatch was on, and all those big fish started working, it was then truly a Fisherman's Paradise. There were trout jumping and splashing at the big flies everywhere. You had to have your line out of the water at nine o'clock. Guys were frantic to get that one last cast, or land a fish before the siren blew. Fortunately, some of the wardens were pretty lenient. It was a gas."

The Paradise was an expensive project to maintain. The original creel limit of two was lowered to one to accommodate the pressure. Later, after Penn State's cyanide spill devastated the project and increasing pollution prevented the food chain's return to its original health, the Commission cut back stocking and eliminated feeding, but permitted unlimited trips. Pure catch-and-release regulations were established and remain in effect.

The Paradise remained a popular place to fish even after pollution devastated Spring Creek. Despite the limited menu of hatches, anglers still had to innovate. "Back in my undergraduate days at PSU, I spent most of my fishing time at the Paradise. Dry fly fishing was limited to midges and terrestrials. Fishing light tippets was necessitated both by the fussiness of the fish and the tiny flies needed to fool them. In the late 1960s and early 1970s, limp 6x and 7x leader material did not exist. Flyfishers back then were a rough and ready group, and we used monofilament sewing thread obtained at department stores. It was about 6x and only tested maybe two-lb. when new. It was the best we had, however, and I caught a lot of good fish using it." Steve Sywensky

Stocking ceased in the 1980s, when surveys found the wild trout population sufficient to rate status as Pennsylvania Class A wild trout water. The decision remains controversial, and both sides have points. The days of 100 trout on Corkers and Honey Bugs are gone, but catching wild trout is more of an accomplishment than hauling in stockies. The Paradise remains a great place to fish.

Fisherman's Paradise furthered fly fishing and quality fishery management more than any other section of water in the world. Thousands of people got their first taste of fly fishing and fly tying there. The project created support for catch and release as anglers saw how good the fishing could be under enlightened regulations. Because the Paradise was accessible to anyone, many more people experienced the possibilities there than at an exclusive private club. The project developed a larger advocacy group for special regulations more quickly than any other water ever has.

"I would like to see the Paradise brought back to what it used to be. There's no question that the Commission could if it wanted. They could stock it, put the dams back in, and manage it catch and release. The Paradise could draw as many people as it used to, if not more. It would be a great educational place, especially if they would get someone to help the anglers. The Commission could create a lot of good will and publicity if they brought back the Paradise. I think it's a shame that they let it go; the Paradise was fun." *George Harvey: Memories, Patterns and Tactics*

The Paradise vaulted Spring Creek into angling limelight. "When I came to Penn State, few anglers fished Spring Creek and other county waters. But Fisherman's Paradise was publicized after it opened, and after that the crowd grew. The fellows would go to the Paradise, keep their limit of two trout, and then fish another part of the stream. Word got around about how good the fishing was, and it wasn't long until fishermen were all over Spring Creek." *George Harvey: Memories, Patterns and Tactics*

Eager anglers built camps along the stream, and a carnival atmosphere pervaded the stream on the opening day of trout season. The influx was as important to Bellefonte merchants as Penn State football is to some State College businesses today.

"Spring Creek had a great name that drew people from all over. There were lots of wild trout, but the stream was also well stocked. People today don't realize how popular the stream was. One year in the early 1940s, we fished below Houserville on opening day. The season opened at 5 AM. in those days. The road was parked bumper to bumper, even though it was still so dark that we had to use a flashlight to find our way around. George Harvey had this stretch to himself on opening day in 1932."

"My exciting times were from the mid thirties through the late forties. That's when I became a bona fide wet fly fisherman. If you had a Royal Coachman and a pair of droppers, you could butcher them. When the hatches came off, you could clean up. I took lots of limits in those days."

"Most people fished bait, but the area was also a hotbed of fly fishing because of the Paradise. When the hatches were on and fish were jumping, you saw more people fishing fly. In-season stocking ceased around Memorial Day. After that there was less pressure, but the season ended July 31. It wasn't until the 1950s that you could fish into August."

"You wouldn't see as much pressure on other local streams. On Penn's Creek, for instance, you could have a half mile of water to yourself. Spring Creek's tributaries weren't fished hard. Thompson and Slab Cabin Runs and Logan Branch had great fishing, but they didn't get the pressure because people wanted to fish the main stream." Joe Humphreys

The masses included a unique set of anglers. In 1934, George Harvey began an unaccredited class in fly tying at Penn State, which became accredited as a full angling class in 1947. Since its inception, thousands of students have enjoyed field trips to Spring Creek. "You could drive into the Penitentiary grounds then, and I often took them to the stretch by parking lot #4. There were some riffles there that were easy to fish with wet flies, and most of the kids could catch a trout or two." George Harvey

Anglers enjoying a May evening downstream from Fisherman's Paradise.

Subsequent classes under George's successors Joe Humphreys, Vance McCullough, and Mark Belden used the Paradise as a training ground. Many angling class graduates became ardent conservationists and credit Spring Creek with helping develop a passion for the outdoors.

At the height of its popularity, Spring Creek was struck down by pollution. Anglers' experiences following the disaster are different than those before. "Spring Creek used to stink to high heaven. I remember one night in the mid-1970s in particular. I arrived at the stream about 7 P.M., anticipating the sulfur hatch that was just starting to re-establish itself. I opened my car door and got a whiff of an intense chemical smell from the water. It was so bad that my eyes began to water. I left quickly for a stretch near Lemont, upstream from the State College sewer and chemical plant discharges. The water in this area had less "body" to it!" Steve Sywensky

Despite the pollution, people still flocked to the stream, if for no other reason than the heavy stocking. Mark Antolosky, son of the late WCO Paul Antolosky, has an inside perspective on Spring Creek. "In-season stockings were almost as bad as opening day. The road between the Paradise and Bellefonte often got so jammed that State Troopers had to direct traffic! Ranks of anglers lined the banks, and, when the trout were dumped in, a volley of rigs was thrown into the stream at them. Dad would drop me off at the Paradise before going on patrol and pick me up at the end of the day. There was always something going on. I learned a lot by watching other flyfishers and really honed my fly fishing skills.

When we wanted to fish a hatch, however, we had to go to Penn's or Fishing Creeks, or Spring Creek's upper water because hatches were nil throughout most of Spring Creek."

My Spring Creek experience began in 1974. When I transferred to Penn State's main campus in the fall, I beat feet to Spring Creek. Despite obvious pollution, it was way off the scale compared to the western Pennsylvania freestone trickles near my home town. Spring Creek harbored more and larger trout in autumn than my home streams did after spring stocking! It looked like a river to me, the mother lode. The stream was still stocked and heavily fished in early season, but summer and fall saw little traffic. Hatches were scant, but even as I began my fly fishing career, Spring Creek began to rebound. I was a fortunate witness.

The transformation began at the nadir of the stream's reputation. In 1977, the day before opening day of trout season, Pennsylvania's Department of Environmental Resources advised the Fish Commission that fish from Spring Creek downstream from Thornton Spring should not be eaten because of pesticide contamination. The issue hit the press. The advisory was posted along the stream, and within a month Spring Creek downstream from the Benner Pike was almost deserted. Unheralded at the time was the completion of the Spring Creek Chapter of Trout Unlimited's Thompson Run project, which dramatically improved water temperatures and quality over

25

Daniel Shields

You can always tell when a hatch is on at Spring Creek.

much of the main stream.

As angling pressure went down and water quality improved, the trout population shot up in size and number. Previously marginal stretches offered excellent sport. Fishing was ridiculously easy. Big dumb wild trout would take dragging dry flies while the angler stood in full view, and it was not unusual to take doubles on a team of wets or nymphs. The Paradise excepted, pressure was limited to a dedicated few, many of whom practiced catch and release. Spring Creek had become, almost overnight, the finest public trout fishery in Pennsylvania.

Fish Commission data supports this claim. A survey of Spring Creek's wild trout population indicated the highest density in Pennsylvania public water. To rate as Pennsylvania Class A Wild Trout Water, a stream has to hold a minimum of 40 lb./acre of wild trout. Some sections of Spring Creek held, and still hold, almost five times as much!

The average size of fish could jade an angler. Anything smaller than a foot was a nuisance, and, when the trout were biting with any enthusiasm, every fourth or fifth fish was 14-inches or better. We dubbed them "Kepone Specials," after the pesticide. Big fish were common during a real flurry. For instance, one evening's short jaunt yielded me a dozen trout, only two of which were smaller than 12-inches. Streamside meetings with other anglers resulted in friendly razzing

and helpful tips rather than confrontation. For me, these were the golden years of Spring Creek fishing. We will never have such fishing on the stream again.

Insect hatches were slow to develop. Consequently, surface activity during peak hatch time did not provide much of a draw for dry fly fishers. An exception was summer terrestrial fishing. Japanese beetles were still plentiful then, and all you had to do to catch a trout was smack a #14 Crowe beetle on the surface. I frequently used up a dozen beetles in a morning before going to work. When fishing slowed, we chummed fish by shaking beetles out of branches overhanging the water.

Nymph fishers had the best action. Even a neophyte could go out and make a haul to brag about. The trout were not leader shy, and just about any rig worked well. Bait men, too, found that they could catch more and bigger trout faster at Spring Creek than anywhere else, and therein lay the seed of disaster.

Although there was an advisory against eating fish from Spring Creek, there was no ban on killing trout. In dilute amounts, Spring Creek's pesticide contaminants are not quick-acting poisons, and, since nobody had died as a result of eating Spring Creek trout, realization dawned that you could eat the fish and feel no immediate ill effect. The anglers' grapevine transmitted word about the great fishing, and the vultures gathered.

A slaughter began, reaching its peak during a strike at Cerro Metals in 1981. The strike coincided

26

with the first part of trout season, and many workers from the plant enjoyed the time off catching Spring Creek trout. Those of us who practiced catch and release watched in dismay as the stream was despoiled. WCO Paul Antolosky told me he estimated over 500 trout larger than 14-inches were killed between The Paradise and Route 550 in two weeks. The greedy behavior of some of the anglers was disgusting. I asked one man why he kept the fish when they were no good to eat. His reply was unforgettable, "I don't eat them, I use them for 'coon bait." Wild trout have more value alive than dead, and this was gross misuse of a resource.

Many anglers and Fish Commission personnel were unhappy about the state of affairs, but little was done because nothing illegal was happening. Finally, in 1982, Frank Zettle, then Regional Vice President of the TU State Council, wrote to Ralph Abele, then Executive Director of the Fish Commission. Frank pointed out the Commission's legal exposure in permitting anglers to take contaminated fish for consumption and suggested that a no-kill regulation would remove the Commission from potential liability. The letter was widely circulated, and in 1983 the Commission adopted a special "Pollution Regulation" that prohibited the killing of trout from Spring Creek.

In 2000, Spring Creek regulations were changed again. The stream is now the Spring Creek Trophy Management Area, and catch and release is currently in effect from Oak Hall to Milesburg. This is a significant change in Commission policy toward Spring Creek because it acknowledged the value of the fishery, not just its pollution. Credit for the new management is largely due to lobbying by the Spring Creek Chapter of Trout Unlimited. Anglers should beware of challenges to this management, and should vigorously resist attempts to change the regulations.

The regulation came just in time. Spring Creek now enjoys a good reputation but cannot be plundered. Improving water quality has made hatches that had been almost extinct offer good sport. Flyrodders again flock to the stream from all parts of North America. The pressure they bring adds another, often dominant element to the Spring Creek angling experience.

Until 1977, pressure concentrated at specific times and places. The Paradise was always busy, and anglers crowded the stocking points outside of the project. At other times, however, much of the stream was lightly fished. Shorter seasons also ensured that Spring Creek trout were undisturbed for months. Additionally, the stream's reputation was poor through most of the latter part of the 20th century. All of this changed in the 1990s.

Spring Creek now has no closed season, and everybody, his brother, uncle and dog knows about the fishery. Guides work the stream from more than 100 miles away! Instead of concentrated pressure at a few spots at key times of the year, there is steady, often heavy traffic every day, excepting the worst days in winter. If you do not see other anglers, it is often because the fishing was or will be better at some other time that day. For example, few people fish on August afternoons because that morning's legion of trico aficionados is taking a siesta. So heavy is pressure that some anglers fish at night to avoid crowds. One hardy soul told me, "It's a pain to night fish in winter because you can't tell if your guides are iced up except by feel!"

As you would expect, Pennsylvania residents are most numerous, but visitors from many states come to sample the fishing. The crowd even includes a sizable Canadian contingent, which travels here early and late season, when northern waters are ice-bound. Many local anglers now seek solitude on less popular waters.

Pressure peaked in the late 1990's, when a spill of unknown origin at the nearby Little Juniata River decimated hatches at that popular stream. Flyrodders deserted the River in droves, and many of the refugees ended up at Spring Creek. Fortunately, the resurgence of insects at the Little Juniata now draws considerable traffic the other way.

There is no predicting where the flock of anglers will land. A pool that gets whipped to a froth three evenings in a row may be deserted the next. No part of the stream escapes for long. On the most "remote" stretch of Spring Creek, you can meet many others also looking for solitude. As my friend George "The Gypsy" Lukas put it, "I used to look at the sky, water, and bugs to tell me when and where to fish. Now I look at the parking lots."

This pressure is a double-edged sword. We all like plenty of water to ourselves. That does not usually happen at Spring Creek. But the stream has to demonstrate popularity to maintain itself in a community whose driving forces are indifferent to the stream's survival.

Pressure from all types of angling comes to a head before the opening of the regular trout season. Spring Creek is one of the few places in Pennsylvania where non-flyfishers can angle for trout at any time of the year. Consequently, the stream plays host to those who otherwise would fish elsewhere and kill their catch. The number of bait and lure anglers dismays some purists, but there is a bright side.

A gratifying number of the bait and spin fishers enjoy catch and release. Mark Nale, a skilled spin

Eric Gansauer fishing some of the Fish & Boat Commission water.

fisherman, keeps copious records of his fishing trips, "I think Spring Creek is number one! I catch 60% of my big trout over 16-inches from the stream, but I only spend 15% of my fishing time there. No other public stream in the state touches Spring Creek for big trout, Erie tribs excepted. The fishing is great because of catch and release, no doubt about it."

Mark has long been a strong advocate for catch and release. Spring Creek is educating others. Recently, I watched a couple of worm fishers work the stretch that I take clients to for fly fishing instruction. I thanked them after I saw them use forceps to release a number of trout without even lifting the fish out of the water. I have seen many flyrodders take less care of their catch. Another bait man came to a Trout Unlimited meeting, where he told the interested assembly how much he enjoyed catch and release. He noticed that fly fishermen did well, and that he was going to try fly fishing. He commented that he did not want the stream to go back to "the old way."

This makes a strong case for no gear restriction. Anglers who otherwise would not have tried catch and release fishing are exposed to the concept at Spring Creek. Many of them become convinced of the value of managing a fishery for quality angling.

Pressure on Spring Creek is a fact of life. Looking for a hole in the crowd is as good a way as any to fish the stream. Fortunately, wherever you find flowing water in Spring Creek, you will find trout.

A Trip Down Spring Creek

Spring Creek's beginning as an intermittent trickle in the swale along Route 322 near the Elks' Country Club near Boalsburg shows little promise of great fishing. Not until Boalsburg, where a couple of springs bubble up from the valley floor, does the stream have permanent flow. Even here, Spring Creek's flow is tenuous, for during dry years, the ground absorbs its flow a short distance downstream.

In past years this was a productive, little-fished stretch. It is still seldom visited, but much less rewarding. When I first fished here, I was amazed at the number and size of the trout in such a small stream. I caught brook trout up to 12-inches and browns larger than that. One acquaintance, Neil Kimmerer of Boalsburg, caught a 19-inch brownie just downstream from the Boalsburg Pike bridge. Trout in the little runs and pools now average much smaller, 4- to 8-inches, with a few larger fish present. Spring Creek through Boalsburg averages 4- to 15-feet in width. Water conservation measures could return this stretch to its former quality.

Most anglers reckon the hamlet of Oak Hall as the fishery's real beginning. In this crossroads community, Spring Creek more than doubles in size from the influx of numerous springs and a major tributary, Cedar Run. With added flow, the stream quickly takes

Daniel Shields

A trout rises on a misty morning in Lemont.

on a different character. Average width is twice that of the Boalsburg water, and depth increases, too. The trout, too, increase in size and run from 6- to 10-inches, with bigger fish more numerous than upstream.

Some of the larger ones are trophies. I got an excited call one fall day from Dave Carson, who urged me to see a big one near his house. I could not see the whole fish because half of it was under a boulder. Dave measured the boulder later and calculated the massive trout's length at 28-inches.

The first few hundred yards of Spring Creek in Oak Hall are posted against public fishing, as is Cedar Run. Access begins at the bridge on Boalsburg Road and continues, almost uninterrupted, from there to Spring Creek's confluence with Slab Cabin Run, about three miles downstream. These upper miles are pleasant to fish, but parking is a problem.

The stream's character downstream from Oak Hall is that of a typical meadow limestoner. Small pools alternate with short, gentle riffles, and stream-side brush and weeds offer casting challenges. In Lemont, gradient steepens, and Spring Creek hurries through a suburban setting. Riffles are common, and there is even some pocket water. Well-tended back yards and shade trees border the stream, and residents will inquire about your luck. Some of the locals fish, and piscatorial motives lurk behind their friendly queries!

Spring Creek exits Lemont at the Benner Pike,

a noisy end for a pleasant stretch. Here, the effects of urban runoff are immediately apparent. Many formerly productive pools are now choked with road gravel, but trout hold in every hint of cover. Spring Creek Park in Houserville offers a convenient place to access this section. The park water used to afford excellent sport, but has silted and shallowed in recent years. Hopefully, stream improvement work will restore lost quality.

The confluence with Slab Cabin Run marks the next major jump in Spring Creek's size. Slab Cabin has itself doubled in volume from the influx of Thompson Run shortly before joining the main stream. Their mingled waters meet Spring Creek a few hundred yards downstream from Spring Creek Park.

With the new water, Spring Creek is no longer a small stream. In this stretch, it averages 15- to 40-feet wide, and temperatures remain trout-friendly all summer. Gradient drops further, and this section of the stream is the flattest of the main stem. It would be delicious to write about a magnificent meadow fishery, where trout dimple the water in slicks and glides throughout gentle meanders overhung with willows. Such was formerly the case, but not now.

Willows, picturesque bends and pools still beckon, but this is the most sorely afflicted part of Spring Creek. Town, campus, and farm runoff shock this section with sediment and lawn and agricultural chemicals. Deep pools have silted in, and spots that

29

The Benner Spring section gets intense pressure.

Daniel Shields

used to offer shelter, feeding, and holding lies are now buried. As the stream bottom fills, water is forced into the banks, hastening erosion in a relentless destruction of this formerly beautiful area. Despite the decay, trout hold wherever they can, and it is a tribute to Spring Creek's quality that sport in this reach is superior to many other streams. Paradoxically, the seclusion of this stretch lends itself to poaching, which depresses the trout population. In addition to human predators, blue herons find this, the least fished part of the stream, a haven from anglers' interruption. The largest flock of herons that I have seen was in Houserville.

With loss of habitat, hatches and trout decline. Small flies predominate, and midges make up the bulk of aquatic offerings. The average size of the trout suffers, too. 6- to 10-inches is the norm, smaller than those in other limestone streams of comparable size. Bigger ones are present, but not in their former numbers. A bank stabilization project executed by the Spring Creek Chapter of Trout Unlimited under the leadership of Bob Carline halted some of the decline, but trout populations have been slow to rebound.

Silt persists as the stream winds through Houserville and into Struble's Meadow. Another Trout Unlimited bank stabilization project here halted deterioration of fine water. Nonetheless, Struble's Meadow is a shadow of the fishery that once revealed to George Harvey "eight or nine hundred rising trout." Some of the water in this vicinity is posted.

Spring Creek exits Houserville downstream from Struble's Meadow at a sharp bend by the UAJA sewage plant. This area contains several new developments for the stream. One is obvious: the sewage plant. Less apparent is the influx of water from Big Hollow's underground flow. Plenty of seeps and springs are present, and they ameliorate the sewage plant's effects to some degree.

Water is faster and the streambed rocky here. Some of the silt has dropped out, and this section is healthier than the flat water upstream. The better cover and hatches support more and bigger trout. Anglers know it, too, and this part of Spring Creek gets hammered. Rock Road parallels the stream, and eager flyrodders will road-fish, looking for unoccupied spots. Such spots are few because of the proximity to town and the high proportion of anglers among streamside residents. Flyfisher's Paradise fly shop conducts fly fishing schools here, adding extra bursts of pressure.

Rock Road leaves Spring Creek at Rock, a limestone outcropping and site of one of the earliest settlements along the stream. Benner Spring's impoundment is a short distance downstream from the parking lot. The two mile stretch of water downstream from Rock is one of the fishery's hot spots.

Fish grow big here because of a curious combination of spring and effluent flow. Springs and hatchery discharges cool the stream in summer, and, combined with the UAJA discharge, keep winter temperatures slightly warmer. Nutrients in the water from hatchery and human waste supercharge the food chain. The trout here are as large as you will encounter on public water in the eastern United States, a virtue that has been widely publicized.

The biggest brook, brown and rainbow trout that I have caught at Spring Creek have come from the Benner Spring stretch. I seldom reveal information like this for fear of drawing extra attention to a particular piece of water, but it would be hard to cram more pressure into this area than it already gets. The fishing is relentless, winter and summer. Only the hatchery outflow at Fisherman's Paradise sees more traffic on a rod/surface area basis.

Other reasons for the popularity of Benner Spring are its proximity to town and pleasant surroundings. Benner Spring is in the upper end of Rockview Penitentiary grounds, and this part of the watershed is little developed. Fauna testifies to this as Anglers frequently see black bear in this locale. Road access is from the parking lot at Rock or via Shiloh Road, which services the hatchery and intersects the Benner Pike near the Nittany Mall. From these points, however, one must walk, and only the reach upstream from Fisherman's Paradise offers as much walk-in fishing. The closest threats to this section are runoff from the Univer-

sity Park Airport and development along I-99.

Spring Creek near Benner Spring averages 30- to 50- feet wide. Gradient is moderate, with more pools and runs than riffles. Hatches used to be so poor here that I remember my joy at seeing just one mayfly. Bugs have now rebounded enough to yield decent sport, and selective surface feeding now occurs where no trout rose in 1980.

The mileage between Benner Spring and Fisherman's Paradise is the most remote on the stream. Anglers wishing to fish this water must remember that Rockview Penitentiary posts a short piece of water a half mile downstream from Benner Spring hatchery. To fish all this water from one access point is not possible, and flyrodders who wish to reach the lower "Pen" water must do so from the Paradise. Walking will not leave the crowds behind because everyone with energy fishes the place. I often see more people fishing upstream from the Paradise than in the project itself!

The Paradise offers exceptional fishing for such a high-pressure place. It is often good under crummy water conditions. No-wading restrictions work in anglers' favor at such times because trout are less prone to spook in murky water and move to the banks where they are easily reached. Other times are not as easy because Paradise trout are well educated. One angling buddy, Rege Nickles, told me that he cast to a trout

A boulder in the canyon stretch of Spring Creek creates good trout cover.

Spring Creek is a large stream just upstream from its confluence with Bald Eagle Creek.

that looked at his fly, then swam downstream a few feet and waited to see if it dragged by the time it reached the fish's new lie! Other flyrodders have told me that they have seen trout refuse live insects for fear of fraud.

There used to be a big spring at the Paradise, but it is now diverted through the hatchery. The hatchery outflow releases into the remnants of the former women's stream, now a shallow ditch at the downstream end of the facility. Barely fifty yards long, this is a hotspot when the rest of the stream is flooded. There are usually a lot of trout here, and I often see a half dozen flyrodders flogging this little stretch of water. The best time to fish the outflow is when hatchery personnel clean settling pond screens. The fish go nuts over the offal. Chunks of dead trout, decayed pellets, and other delicacies are excitedly inhaled by otherwise fastidious feeders. The trouts' glee would grieve Halford and Marinaro if they were alive today and makes a mockery of the popular conception of trout as selective gourmands.

A number of smaller springs also enter the stream at the Paradise, and the stream's character changes, too. Gradient steepens, and riffles become more numerous. Spring Creek from the Paradise to Bellefonte has the best structure of any part of the stream, and dozens of small springs sustain the trout during drought. The trout average 10- to 13-inches, with many bigger fish present, and it is hard to exaggerate their numbers. They have plenty to feed on, too. No other part of the stream has better hatches.

This magnificent three-mile section is the most fisherman-friendly part of Spring Creek. Road access is convenient and parking spots are plentiful. The Fish and Boat Commission owns a large chunk of the most desirable water, and local residents are gracious hosts. Stream width runs anywhere from 15- to 60-feet, and there is a great riffle/pool ratio. Surroundings not pristine but pleasant nonetheless. Small houses and fishing camps dot the banks, interspersed with brushy woodlots. Of course, anglers are drawn here like moths to light. I have seen people fishing so close to each other in this stretch that their back casts crossed. It can be hard to find a parking spot at prime time, and I have even seen tour buses bring in groups of anglers. Altercations occur, and landowners and anglers alternately laugh at and lament the antics. "I was below the Paradise one day, and two men kicked up spray as they ran through the water to beat me to a spot." Steve Sywensky

Anglers should exercise good behavior on Spring Creek. Although much of the water is publicly owned, a lot is not. Only the incredible generosity of landowners permits access to many nice spots. Flyrodders can help keep private land open to public fishing access by not blocking driveways, by picking up litter, and by keeping noise to a minimum. If landowners ask for cooperation, give it to them immediately, without argument.

Spring Creek doubles in volume at Bellefonte with the addition of Logan Branch and the Big Spring. With this infusion, the stream runs cold and strong to Milesburg. Maximum width in this lower water reaches close to 90-feet in places. There are loads of fish, and hatches are excellent. Access is tricky, because parking spots are few and often full. This part of the stream would be secluded but for the ever-present crowd of anglers, many of whom walk from Bellefonte or Milesburg. Spring Creek here is large enough for kayaks, which create recreational chaos at times. Trees and brush line much of the stream in this section, but their shade also shields poachers, who hurt this stretch.

Spring Creek's end is more dramatic than its beginning. A series of rock ledges just upstream from the confluence with Bald Eagle Creek churns the full flow into a stretch of rapids far louder than the gentle murmuring heard in Boalsburg. Even after joining with Bald Eagle, Spring Creek continues to be productive, for its cooling water rejuvenates the stream it feeds, and its limestone water neutralizes acid mine drainage as far away as the West Branch of the Susquehanna.

Hatches

"The hatches on Spring Creek were incredible. There were Hendricksons, Isonychia, numerous different caddis, sulfurs, and more! The Green Drake Hatch came up as far as Struble's Meadow. Upstream, there wasn't foliage along the stream to shelter the flies. I was below there one night, and helped a fellow land a 25-inch native brown trout. He called for me to come with my net, and I went down and got in the water. When I lifted the fish out of the water, it stuck out both sides of the net. It must have weighed five or six pounds. There were clouds of flies, and the trout were taking them all over. I didn't have a Green Drake, and all I used was a big dry fly. I caught only one 13-inch fish. I must have caught it by accident." Joe Humphreys

"The hatches on Spring Creek were tremendous. Sometimes the water would get so covered with flies that — well there were just a mass of flies on the water. A trout could rise and get more than one fly at a time. The fish would hang just below the surface and gulp the flies." *George Harvey: Memories, Patterns and Tactics*

Many of Spring Creek's original aquatic insect hatches were polluted into oblivion by Penn State's cyanide spill in 1956. Grannoms and green drakes, which with their profusion once thrilled flyrodders, are gone. As water quality declined, so did the food chain. By the mid-1970s Spring Creek was a poor place to match a hatch. The only fishable aquatic hatch in most of the stream was a little black midge, locally

Greg Hoover

Midge: Spring Creek plays host to many species of these small flies. They vary widely in size and color.

nicknamed "the sewer fly," after its tenacious ability to live in what many felt Spring Creek had become. Other hatches were either extinct or existed in painfully sparse numbers.

Fortunately, the water upstream from the Benner Pike retained enough quality to nurture populations of important aquatic species. These flies, together with donations of insects brought in from other waters by concerned flyfishers, served as a base from which Spring Creek began to reclaim some status as a bug factory. These days, the stream boasts enough fishable hatches to fill a hatch chart. Better yet, the trout work the hatches!

Flyrodders can fish a hatch on Spring Creek as early as New Year's Day, weather and water conditions permitting. Sewer flies hatch all year: only the worst winter weather shuts them down completely. These are tiny flies — #28 is not too small — and their size causes complaint by those of us whose eyesight is not equal to our enthusiasm. Any small black dry fly offers a chance during this hatch. Griffith's Gnats and appropriate pupal patterns also work well.

In February, the miniscule flies are joined by a bewildering array of other midges and the first little blue-winged olives. Black midges as large as #20 emerge, as do brown midges in #20 - 24, light olive midges in #24, and dark olive midges ranging from #18 to #24. The smaller flies far outnumber the larger, but trout will work the bigger ones. For instance, when large dark olive midges are on the water in quantity, they bring up more and larger fish than do the smaller flies.

To be honest, I am unsure if the different colors represent different species, genders within a species, emergent flies, or returning egglayers. Sometimes, the answer is obvious because you can see the bugs flying up from the stream. At such times, it pays to try pupal imitations as well as dries. When picking a pattern, choose size first and then color.

Blue-winged Olive spinner

Midges can make trout persnickety. One of the best midge fishermen on the stream in recent years was Dave Brown, stationed (not by accident) at the U.S. Army recruiting office in State College. Dave worked like a dog to get his midge patterns and tactics right, only to find that, despite considerable success, he was unable to score all of the time. Dave went to great lengths to concoct different rigs and patterns and was constantly on the lookout for new answers.

A different "hatch" begins in mid-February, but does not show on the surface. White suckers spawn, and their roe provides more solid fare than midges. Trout cue up downstream from spawning suckers, taking drifting eggs and nymphs the hosenoses kick out with their nuptial antics. Trout greet dislodged aquatics with enthusiasm, but eggs are often seized with outright abandon.

Anglers have capitalized on this opportunity for decades. Sucker Spawn, a pattern first popularized at Fisherman's Paradise, has been fished there since at least the 1960s. I read about the fly in a little article the late Paul Antolosky contributed to the *Pennsylvania Angler*. For some reason, the fly stuck in my mind, and when I took up fly fishing, the Sucker Spawn was one of the first patterns I tied. The fly went a long way to boosting my confidence as a tyro fly fisherman.

The Paradise was one of only three places open to winter trout fishing in the Keystone State at that time. Sucker spawn provided one of the high points of the season there. The Paradise was stocked in those days, and it was always fun to try to catch a "Pennsylvania Grand Slam" — brook, brown, rainbow, and palomino trout. The first large trout I caught on fly were taken on Sucker Spawn at the Paradise, and many other anglers can make the same claim.

Sucker Spawn is best fished dead drift, on the bottom. Takes are often vigorous, and it is possible to rack up a good score out of one pocket. A handicap is

that action is often localized and unpredictable. At times, the fly works well on the entire stream. More frequently, however, action is centered in a few choice locations, which change from day to day. The activity persists into early May, but by then trout focus more attention on other events.

Little blue-winged olive (BWO) begin to show up in late February, and anglers greet them as a sign that winter will not last forever. The BWOs also offer relief from the problems associated with fishing midges. Some of the BWOs run as large as #16, but #18 - #20 are more common. Unfortunately, the best hatches often coincide with lousy weather and water. In flyrodders' favor, trout like BWOs and will often take them when midging. This enables anglers to get away with fishing a fly larger than the ones the fish are actually taking. Another useful tactic is to play off both hatches. This calls for a tandem rig with a BWO dry trailed by a midge pupa on a short dropper. When doing so, you can fish two hatches at once, at different levels.

Little BWOs linger into May, but as spring progresses, their emergence is spotty and shifts into late evening. Trout remain tuned to them, and work even sparse hatches in a fashion that can fool dry fly veterans. The small, dark flies often go unnoticed at dusk and in the excitement generated by larger, more visible flies. My suspicion is that weather makes some years better than others for late spring olive emergences. Whatever the reason, bring BWOs in different sizes to Spring Creek!

Mid-April sometimes sees a gap in Spring Creek's hatches, with one frustrating exception. Tiny white midges, little bigger than a dot, are frequently the only surface game. Their evening ovipositing flights bring up fish in flat water, where slow currents and finicky trout make matching this hatch a pain. By this time, dry fly anglers on Spring Creek are itching to fish something larger than a #18.

Crane Flies

Relief comes when yellow and orange crane flies begin hatching in mid-April. Most crane fly species are not aquatic, but Spring Creek is home to a couple that are. These flies resemble goofy mosquitoes, without the snout, and their size, color, and life cycle makes them allies of flyfishers and dedicated bait men.

George Harvey told me that crane fly larvae were one of his favorite baits before he became totally committed to fly fishing. The larvae are nasty looking things whose appearance earns nicknames like waterworms and jelly worms. Trout love them for the square meal they represent. Crane fly nymphs produce all year, although the best time to fish them is prior to and during emergence. Walt's Worm and Casual Dress nymphs in #8 - 18 imitate crane fly larvae.

Crane fly adults are beautiful compared to their larvae. It is hard to believe the dainty flies come from such ugly nymphs. Their yellow or orange bodies show up well, to the relief of midge fishers' strained eyes, and they have an appealingly difficult time getting off the water. Dries like Steve Sywensky's Crane Fly work well for this hatch. Another productive way to fish crane fly adults is with wet flies like Tup's Indispensable or Sulfurs, which represent drowned bugs.

Like mayflies, aquatic crane flies return to the water to oviposit. On occasion, the flights are strong enough to prompt surface feeding. Orange-bodied Crane Fly patterns score at such times, but remember that trout often switch to midges or olives if they are present in quantity at the same time. It pays to check the water!

Within days of the first crane flies, Spring Creek reinforces its hatches with a couple of caddisfly species. From this point of the season until late October, a variety of caddisflies provide angling opportunities on the surface, bottom, and points between. The different species peak at different times, but even dog days in August see a few caddisflies flitting about. As an added bonus, trout become so accustomed to eating the bugs that they sometimes take imitations when naturals are few.

The two caddisfly species appearing first provide the most concentrated Trichoptera action of the season. The most numerous is a #16, tan-winged, light olive-bodied fly. Its frequent companion is a #14, tan-winged, golden olive-bodied fly that, though less numerous, also brings fish to the surface. Both of these flies are widespread in Pennsylvania.

Weather is a key factor in timing the emergence of these flies. Cool days produce afternoon hatching, while warm days stimulate morning emergences. Regardless of the air temperature, these flies make a

Spring Creek has many different caddis.

fuss on the surface. When I raised these caddisflies in an aquarium, I was amazed at their acrobatics. Their vigor aids dry fly anglers when trout rise hurriedly to the struggling insects. However, this can be a double-edged sword when fish key on skittering flies. It's darn near impossible to make an imitation hop like the natural. When I twitch my rig to mimic a jumping fly, I usually get incredible drag and spooked trout.

Caddisfly cripples make for easier pickin's. This could be a reason for the success of Elk Hair Caddis patterns during this hatch. This imitation's splayed wing gives the impression of a natural whose wings are stuck in the surface film. Trailing shuck patterns also work well, as do Delta Wing Caddis. An effective pattern I devised is a Hair Delta Wing, with and without a shuck. This pattern floats better than the hackle tip variety and gives a good silhouette.

Olive-colored larval imitations of this caddisfly catch fish, but pupae can be the best subsurface ticket. Many caddisfly larvae hide under rocks throughout much of their cycle and are not readily available food. The pupae, however, expose themselves during emergence, and nature curses them with a signal singularly visible to trout eyes. Nailing down the visual trigger that prompts trout to take the pupae caused me problems and no little embarrassment.

Whatever the trout sees in the pupae, it is not the color of the insect. I fished one hatch with a friend who had a stomach pump. Action was good on muskrat nymphs, but we thought a closer imitation would work better. We pumped a fish, and I happened to have an exact imitation, when wet, of the flies we pumped out of the poor trout. We eagerly switched flies and sallied forth to wreak havoc. We caught nothing on "Dan's exact imitations." We re-attached the muskrat nymphs and were back in action.

For the next few seasons, I tried different colors of pupae, but none worked as well as muskrat nymphs or any other flies friends were using. For in-

35

stance, I ran into Paul Rebarchak on the stream one day, and he was having great success on a Gray Pupa while I caught only trees and rocks with every other color. Then, one day on Bald Eagle Creek, when the same flies were hatching, I saw a different colored caddisfly pop up in front of me. I grabbed it and lo! There was the same caddisfly, but its wings were wrapped around it, making it a visible pale gray, even though body color was olive. Much has been written about Trichoptera pupae and their sheath of air bubbles. Those on Spring Creek are no exception, and pupal patterns dressed to mimic this outfish "Dan's exact imitations."

Sulfur spinner

Late afternoons and evenings see these caddisflies returning to lay eggs. The larger ones are more obvious. They return earlier, dipping and dancing while ovipositing. Smaller caddisflies are less noticeable, as they fly low and fast over the water. Trout rise to both, but the smaller flies provide more consistent action. The females' color darkens after emergence, and a grayish-tan winged, dark olive-bodied pattern matches the flies well. Surface feeding on egglaying Trichoptera is often misread because anglers' eyes are drawn to larger, brighter flies in failing light. From pupae to egglayers, caddisflies are exciting and challenging hatches to fish. But they are overshadowed by Spring Creek's most beloved hatch.

Sulfurs usher in the height of Spring Creek's season. Pennsylvania flyrodders' favorite insects, the sulfurs are several species of mayflies somewhat similar in appearance. The sulfurs' popularity is guaranteed by the timing. No other time of the year has the combination of air and water temperatures so conducive to our sport. Sulfurs enhance this attribute with a long hatch period, dependability, and opportunities provided by all stages of their life cycle.

The first sulfur to appear is known historically as the light Hendrickson. Spring Creek's fecund waters grow this fly to a size larger than other waters: almost a #12. I have seen them on the water as early as April 18, but the first reliable fishing hatches usually do not occur until early May. Curiously, the nymph of this species is almost black, and it always amazes me how such a light fly can emerge from such a dark nymph. Male duns have a pronounced greenish-yellow cast, while females are yellow.

Successful Sulfur Dun patterns are legion, and it pays to carry different imitations on Spring Creek. High-riding standard styles work best at the beginning of the emergence period and after dark, when their visibility aids anglers' vision. Later in the season, low-riding flies like Comparaduns, Cutwings, and Para-

chutes take finicky fish. No one pattern is consistent, and experimentation with different styles, sizes, and colors is the best way to avoid frustration.

Productive Sulfur Nymph patterns are numerous, too. Popular ones include the time-honored Pheasant Tail as well as a host of dubbed fur-bodied flies.

Spring Creek's most numerous sulfur is the pale evening dun, #16 in size. Males are yellow, and females have a pronounced orange cast to their bodies. Nymphs are light tan and spinners dark tan. The evening spinner flights are a sight to behold. Flies are so thick that an insect fog seems to form over prime riffles. Anglers fishing during these flights get spinners in their ears and behind their glasses, and rods and waders become speckled with egg masses and spent flies.

Trout work sulfur spinners with an intensity that can make one frantic just when deliberation is most important. Rising fish will hold in feeding lanes inches wide, and flyrodders must use supreme concentration when casting to such a small target zone, not an easy task during the last minutes of daylight. Compounding the problem is that spinner flights do not occur over the same riffle every evening. The riffle that had a massive flight one night might host few flies the next, while a couple of riffles away there might be a huge swarm.

Little sulfurs (#18) also appear on Spring Creek but are not as important as the bigger species. It pays to carry imitations, however, because they often hatch in numbers sufficient to trigger selectivity. Having had many humbling experiences with little sulfurs, my conclusion is that trout often key on emergers when working this hatch. Little sulfur nymphs are light, yellowish tan, and adults are yellow and orange for males and females, respectively.

Like other mayflies, sulfurs hatch during the most comfortable time of the day. Consequently, warm days see evening hatches and cool days see daytime emergences. In warm weather, one can expect a good

Orange Cahill

evening hatch and spinner fall, with corresponding lighter ones in the morning.

In mid-May, a brighter mayfly begins to emerge. These are orange and yellow light Cahills, which have to be the prettiest mayflies of all. Most common sizes are #12-14, but the occasional larger one pops up. A nice feature about this hatch is that, while peaking in early June, it persists until October. Like late season insects on other waters, even a sparse hatch can bring some fish up. Nymphs of this fly are brownish tan, and spinners are creamy yellow.

Early June brings another caddisfly. This fly is difficult to fish successfully, because it emerges sporadically at dark and after. I stumbled on it by luck after a frustrating evening fishing an Orange Cahill to rising trout. The bright flies were easy to spot and fish, but most fish refused them. There were far more rises than the number of Cahills warranted, but I could not solve the problem. My car was parked beside the stream, and as I packed gear away, the dome light attracted several caddis. These insects are #14-16, with grayish tan wings and a cream body.

By mid-June, Spring Creek evening fishing is largely a dusk or after dark affair. Morning activity picks up, however, as water temperatures at that time of day become most comfortable for trout. Caddisflies continue, as do crane flies and a few sulfurs and cahills, but many species are "hatched out" for the year. Fortunately, as the aquatic insects dwindle, terrestrials fill the void.

Terrestrial fishing is excellent on Spring Creek. Almost any kind of ant, beetle or cricket pattern will produce at some time in the summer and early fall. Terrestrial fishing is relatively easy compared to fishing aquatic hatches. You do not have to wait for flies to hatch or guess what stage of the insect the trout are working. Just pick a pattern and try it. If it does not work, try a different size or pattern. You can fish to rising trout or prospect for bankside feeders. A less

conventional way to capitalize on terrestrials is to fish them subsurface. Wet ants are especially effective. Do not let the weather put you off. A former roommate of mine, Tom Kolb, used to fish during the most miserable days of August. He would come home dripping with sweat, but also with good fishing reports.

Trout can be selective to terrestrials, especially when flying ants are on the water. Late summer and early fall always produce a few days of great fishing. As with midges, the most numerous flying ants are the smallest, a #28 black ant that arrives the last week of August.

Terrestrials are not the only summer game. Spring Creek also gets a decent trico hatch. The hatch begins in early July and is in full swing by mid-month. The tricos' small size (#24) is partially compensated by daylight emergence. In low summer flows, trout are easier to see and fish to with the tiny patterns. The trico hatch is spotty by individual day and stretch of stream. It is possible to have great trico fishing while your buddy 100 yards away does not see a rise. Sometimes the action is great, however, with every pool holding plenty of rising trout. Tricos persist well into autumn, and, once the hatch gets going, it is a rare day that does not see some activity.

In addition to tricos, another small summer mayfly provides sport. This one is a #22-24 tiny blue-winged olive dun with a yellowish-olive body.

Summer fishing on Spring Creek is the most predictable of the year. Fishing is best in the morning, often peaking with the trico spinner fall. The warmer the weather, the earlier you should be astream. The trout are usually active, and anglers should recact to what the stream presents them with when selecting flies and tactics. The biggest problems in summer are low water and fish that have been through the anglers' mill.

Late summer also brings more crane flies. These are smaller (#18) and lighter in color than those that hatch in the spring. Emergence is inconsistent, but

Trico spinner

George Daniel

Amidea Daniel enjoys a catch at Fisherman's Paradise.

achieves importance when little else is on the water. Little BWOs also appear in late summer, and continue into fall. They are not as big (#20-24) as early season BWOs, but trout like them just as well.

Sewer flies also continue in the summer, but not as profusely as in winter and early spring. Another midge, a little white dot, begins in late August and hatches into the fall. These are the most numerous flies to appear at that time on Spring Creek. Their small size (#28) is compensated by a long hatch period and dependability.

Fall brings some decent hatches of Trichoptera. Tan Caddis in #16-18 and a larger fly in #14 produce interesting fishing. The latter fly has grayish-tan wings and a dark olive body. The most exciting caddisfly, in theory at least, is the big (#8) orange October caddis. Conventionally thought of as a western species, this fly is widespread in central Pennsylvania. Most activity is nocturnal, but once in a while they surprise daytime anglers. In general, fall caddisfly hatches are spotty. I have had great action one evening and little the next on the same piece of water, even though atmospheric and stream conditions seemed identical. Autumn water levels are usually low, and prospecting tactics with caddisfly imitations produce as does fishing to the rise.

Trout begin spawning in late fall, and their eggs are as eagerly taken as were sucker eggs earlier in the year. Fishing for spawning trout is a reprehensible activity, but action with a clearer conscience can be had by fishing to egg eaters that hold below redds. Sucker Spawn and Glo Bugs are patterns of choice.

In addition to the hatches discussed, a few other flies provide sport at odd times. Gray Fox and March Brown (the two are now taxonomically identical), Blue Quill, Callibaetis, Hexagenia, and large BWOs (#14-16) are the prime mayfly examples. A couple of grannom caddis have also been sighted in recent years. Unfortunately, stoneflies provide very few opportunities on Spring Creek, even though they are present. One stonefly, the early dark, exists in some numbers, but cannot claim the term "dependable hatch." Most of these different insects provided sport in the past, and it is a tribute to the stream that they are still present.

Hatches are fun, but what really grows Spring Creek trout is its supply of freshwater crustaceans and aquatic worms. These critters fill voids between hatches, and only the strongest emergences override trouts' predisposition for them.

Sowbugs are the staff of life for Spring Creek trout. They resemble roly-polies found under rotting logs and are the most common crustacean in the stream. When I used to kill trout, their stomachs always contained at least a few sowbugs, no matter what else was happening. At the height of Spring Creek's

Mark Antolosky demonstrates line control while nymph fishing.

polluted era, sowbugs were almost all the trout had to eat in some stretches. As George "The Gypsy" Lukas told me, "For years, all we fished were sowbug patterns in the weed channels. We'd wait until the stocking trucks were gone for the year, and then we'd have the stream to ourselves. There were no hatches to bother with: The sowbug was king." One of the sowbug's best attributes is that its numbers peak in late summer and early fall, when other food forms are less available. Millions of them can be seen in weed mats at that time of year. Muskrat Nymphs imitate sowbugs very well. Choose a size based on water clarity. Smaller flies work better in low clear water and vice versa.

Freshwater shrimp, or scuds, and crayfish also live in Spring Creek. Spring Creek shrimp are olive in color, and #16-#20 are the most common sizes. They are more numerous than sowbugs in many parts of the stream.

Crayfish are the largest and least plentiful crustacean, in part because their habitat has dwindled as silt clogs the interstices between rocks. I must confess that I have not fished crayfish patterns on Spring Creek, even though I have watched trout chomp on them numerous times. Steve Sywensky has fished them, however, and he reports, "There is no doubt that Spring Creek trout eat them. For instance, I caught a 17-inch brownie on a trico that threw up six large crayfish while I was unhooking it. My best results with crayfish flies come when I fish them dead

drift in murky water, especially in summer. I do not catch lots of trout with them, but the fishes' average size is larger than those I catch with other nymphs. My favorite crayfish imitation is a fairly small, #10-12 fly with a brown back and tan belly."

Spring Creek hosts several species of aquatic worms, from little red tubifex worms to larger ones indistinguishable from worms sold at bait shops. Aquatic worms are one of the few organisms that have benefitted from Spring Creek's increased silt load. During a trash cleanup, some of us pulled a muck-filled tire out of the stream. Paul Rebarchak checked the mud, and excitedly showed the rest of us a handful of worms that would have done the San Juan River proud. Patterns resembling aquatic worms were fished by Paradise regulars like the late Tony Worrick decades before any mention of the San Juan Worm in fly fishing magazines. Imitations work just as well today.

Baitfish are present in Spring Creek, too. The most important of them is the sculpin, which exists throughout the watershed. Shenk's Sculpin is my favorite imitation for this odd fish. I have tried many different colors and sizes of this excellent fly, and rate #6-8 black ones the best.

If Spring Creek does not have the range of aquatic insects and other food forms other waters have, there is still plenty to keep flyrodders busy. I hope that future improvements in water quality add to this list!

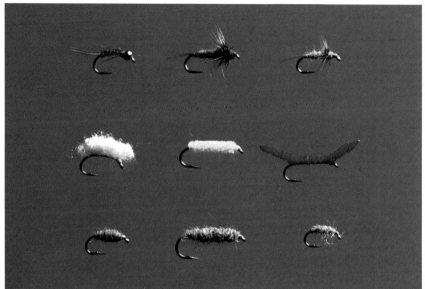

Productive nymphs for Spring Creek: top to bottom, left to right:

Bead Head Pheasant Tail, Dark Sulphur, Light Sulphur, Sucker Spawn, Green Weenie, San Juan Worm, Muskrat Nymph, Walt's Worm, Olive Shrimp.

Nelson Haines

Tactics

Ron Evans and I fished the sulfur hatch one evening below the Paradise. I had bragged about how many fish I was catching on nymphs during the hatch, and at the time wondered why someone would want to fish anything else. Ron fished nymphs, but preferred using dries when possible. "Well, I warned him," I thought as we started fishing. I expected to put on a show, but was I wrong. I nymphed a prime piece of water that I knew well, with scant results. Every time I looked up, however, Ron's rod was bent. My ego deserved the blow; Spring Creek had given me another lesson.

Tactics that work well on other eastern limestone streams also work on Spring Creek. As important as tactics is the angler's state of mind. As my anecdote illustrates, a rigid game plan does little to ensure success. The most successful flyrodders are also the most flexible. The best Spring Creek anglers fish a variety of tactics and delight in experiment.

Dead drift nymph fishing is the most consistent fly fishing method for catching Spring Creek trout. There is so much subsurface life that I sometimes wonder why the trout bother to rise. There good hatches with plenty of drifting nymphs, and some feed, like sowbugs, is only available subsurface. A good nymph fisher seldom gets skunked, even when other methods are working well.

A true dead drift is difficult to achieve while maintaining contact with flies, but attempts to do so yield results. On one occasion, I watched a nymph fisher work a pocket. I detected subtle drag in his presentation, and it showed up all the better because of the indicators he had strung on his leader. I stepped in after he quit the spot, and, taking care to achieve a dead drift with no indicator, took a trout.

There are two points here, and neither of them is my expertise — there are too many witnesses to the contrary. The first is, of course, achieving a dead drift. The second is not to use indicators as a crutch. They are very useful, even necessary in many circumstances, but should be selected and fished properly. If used incorrectly, they can work against you, causing drag and a false sense of complacency. Think of indicators as tools in a toolbox, chosen according to the job at hand.

Weight is critical. Many flyfishers abhor using weight and its effects on casting, but good weighting helps achieve a good drift. It pays to experiment with different combinations of weighted and unweighted flies with and without weight on the leader.

Dead drifting is most effective, but moving nymphs work on occasion. During caddis hatches, pupal imitations fished with a swing sometimes elicit a strike. I have taken trout that chased swung flies all the way to the surface, although too active a presentation usually turns trout off. When swinging flies, you can usually obtain better results by swinging flies up from the bottom instead of across current.

Currents can render dead drifting impossible, but may not spell failure. During sulfur hatches, for instance, there are so many bugs swimming in the water that *slight* drag may not matter. Also, many nymph fishers occasionally catch trout when picking up for their next cast. Nobody is sure why this happens. Maybe the fish follows the nymph during its drift and grabs it when it starts to escape. Perhaps the pickup occurs at the trout's feeding lie. So while a dead drift is desirable, it is not an absolute.

Productive streamers and wet flies for Spring Creek: top to bottom, left to right:

Sulphur Wet, Caddis Pupa, Wet Ant, Orange Cahill Wet, White Shenk Minnow, Black Shenk Sculpin, Black Woolly Bugger.

Nelson Haines

Sight fishing is another nymphing tactic that works. This challenging game is often equated to hunting. Spring Creek's profusion of trout makes it relatively easy to locate trout for sight nymphing. Stalking and casting without spooking the fish is more difficult. Maintaining a dead drift and detecting the strike is even harder. Beware when using indicators for sight nymphing! Many times I have had trout take a fly without moving the indicator. When sight fishing with an indicator, use the indicator to locate the fly, then watch the fly or its location for any hint of movement.

Prior to the resurgence of hatches on Spring Creek, nymph fishing was superior to all other methods. Terrestrials and sewer flies excepted, little existed for trout to rise to over many miles of water. Frequently, underwater action was incredible with no discernible signal to frenzied feeding activity. Pressure was so light that I used 7 1/2-foot leaders with 2x Maxima for tippet. Now I have to go to longer leaders with 4- or 5x soft tippet and fluorocarbon tippets in low clear water.

Wet fly fishing is an enigma through lack of devotees. It is not as productive as nymph fishing, but still has its moments. Wets fished on Spring Creek are most productive when drifted naturally with the current. This is difficult to do and detect strikes at the same time. Strike indicators can help when playing this game. Wets can be fished with nymphs and/or dries on tandem rigs.

Swinging wets is a tricky proposition. It is easy to give too much motion to the flies, yet I have seen fish follow and take wets swung clear across the creek. Usually, however, more subtle swings work better. As with nymphs, the best swing brings flies up through the current rather than across it. A flyrodder must have a good gauge of what water to fish with swung wets, and it is hard to develop that talent. Few anglers are masters at swinging wets, and I am not one of them.

Dapping droppered wets during caddis hatches and ovipositing flights is a lot of fun. A team of flies is employed and the tail fly acts as an anchor from which the flyrodder daps the middle and hand flies. This technique is limited in application because it usually requires a close approach from upstream.

Many anglers use tandem rigs on Spring Creek. This tactic involves attaching a nymph or wet fly to a dry fly with a dropper. The dry fly then acts as a strike indicator with the added attraction of fooling a fish. This is not "pure" nymph or wet fly fishing, but the majority of trout taken on such rigs come on the sunk fly. The key to fishing tandem rigs is selecting the right dropper length. In most cases, the correct choice will put the sunk fly at or near the bottom, but drifting the dropper fly within a few inches of the dry pays off handsomely on many occasions.

Streamers also produce at Spring Creek. Woolly Buggers fished down and across are the most popular fly/method combination employed. This tactic works best in murky water, and a growing number of anglers look forward to fishing 'Buggers after a rain. In low water, it is exciting to fish 'Buggers upstream, retrieving with the current. You will get lots of follows and short hits, but hookups will be few in comparison to the number of fish that chase the fly.

Sculpins bounced on the bottom *a la* Ed Shenk work as well as or better under more water conditions than 'Buggers. They are harder to fish than 'Buggers, however, because they are best fished weighted with lead eyes and/or shot at the head and fished with a leader long enough to keep them down. Such a rig is

Productive dry flies for Spring Creek: top to bottom, left to right:

Orange Cahill, Sulphur, Dan's Hair Delta Wing Caddis, Crane Fly, Letort Cricket, Sulphur Spinner, Crowe Beetle.

Nelson Haines

no picnic to cast and control, especially on upstream presentations, but it does hold the fly on the bottom and allow jigging.

When dark streamers do not yield a strike, try a white or chartreuse one. You can fish Shenk White Minnows and Sculpins, White Marabous, and chartreuse 'Buggers like dark streamers. Light streamers do not show up as well as dark streamers in muddy water, however, which limits their effectiveness.

As Spring Creek's hatches improved, so did its dry fly fishing. Today, dries are often more effective than sunk flies, if not as consistent. Matching the hatch while fishing to the rise is the most common tactic, as it is on other limestone streams. Imitation is a game we all like to play, but, regardless of pattern, achieving a drag free presentation is of paramount importance. The trout are pressured into extreme drag consciousness.

Spring Creek hammers the drag lesson home. For instance, guide Doug Wennick had clients fail to raise trout during a hatch. The clients' casting was accurate, but leaders were allowed to straighten. When Doug explained drag and what caused it, his clients understood the concept, but told him that drag was not an issue on stocked trout in their home stream! The best way to combat drag is to use a George Harvey style leader and fish it with a slack leader cast.

Fishing the water with dries also works well at Spring Creek. You can prospect with imitations of any hatch — even midges — and enjoy success. The trick is to read the water well and remember that the smaller the fly, the closer to the feeding lie you must cast. A better prospecting game is summer terrestrial fishing. I like to start out with a large ant, beetle, or cricket, going smaller if I have to. Large flies are easier to fish

than small ones, and, if the trout will take them you can fish more effectively and take larger fish.

Even the best tacticians fare poorly, however, if they do not follow good stream stategy. Choosing when to fish is often more important than choosing tactics or flies. Fortunately, Spring Creek is helpful, at least with density of its trout population and water temperatures. Anglers know the fish are there, with every spot that looks good holding trout. Most of the time, too, some spot on the stream offers water at a temperature conducive to feeding trout at some point during the day. A good recommendation is to go out at a time of day most comfortable for the time of year. In winter, try the middle of the day, when temperatures are warmest. In summer, fish early, before heat makes you want something to drink more than go fishing. In less extreme weather, be prepared to fish all day so as to not miss any flurry of bugs and/or feeding.

Tackle for Spring Creek is best matched to the angler's choice of tactics. If fishing small dries is your only game, 3- and 4-weight rods will suffice. If you like to fish a variety of techniques, 5- and 6-weight rods are best. A long rod will help with presentation. At no place on the main stream do I feel the need to go any shorter than a 9-foot rod.

But the best thing to remember about Spring Creek fishing is that no matter how technical we make it, or how scientifically we analyze trouts' behavior, feeding patterns, etc., it is still fishing.

I was at the Paradise's upper parking lot pool one summer day. The weather was hot, the water low and clear. A few fish made almost imperceptible dimples to midges in the flat water, and these trout are among the smartest in the stream. As I ruefully contemplated my failure with a couple of midge patterns, a rookie angler started fishing. He struggled out a cast, and his fly plunked down a few feet from the bank. "Just like my first trips," I sympathized. Unlike my first trips, or the one in question for that matter, he immediately caught a trout, and then another. He was really smacking the water with that fly. I could hear it plop a hundred feet away. The harder he whacked it down, the better it seemed to work. I have learned to swallow fishing pride quickly, so I begged him to show me his fly. It was a #10 Green Weenie.

Flies

Spring Creek trout see more different imitations than I do, and I work in a fly shop. This results in many amusing incidents like the above episode. For instance, Jim Brady stopped in one day and enthused about his success with a Royal Coachman wet fly. And during the 1999 drought, Brockway flyfisher Curt Hoffman enjoyed good fishing in the low clear water with Charlie Meck's invention, Patriot attractor dries. I have also witnessed success with bass flies and west coast steelhead flies. Do not rule any pattern out. On one memorable occasion, I caught a trout on a #2 Dahlberg Diver!

One reason for these circumstances is the capricious nature of trout and our sport. Another is fishing pressure. The first anglers to fish over trout with a "new" pattern usually do well. Trout accustom rapidly to fraud, however, and become almost impossible to fool repeatedly on the same flies. In extreme cases, you can sometimes score simply by trying a fly other anglers have not.

Fortunately, wacky flies are not always the best patterns to employ on Spring Creek. Far more trout are caught on conventional imitations of common food forms. My fly boxes contain hundreds of different choices for Spring Creek, but I fish relatively few of them. Those flies, plus favorites of friends, make a formidable arsenal of offerings. An assortment of these flies in different sizes will take trout most of the time.

Nymphs

BWO Nymph #16-20, Cahill Nymph #12-14, Crawfish #8-12, Dark Sulphur #12-16, Deep Sparkle Caddis Pupa #14-18, Green Weenie #10-16, Light Sulphur #14-18, Midge pupa #16-28, Muskrat #10-22, Olive Caddis Larva #12-18, Olive Shrimp #14-20, Otter #10-22, Pheasant Tail #12-20, San Juan Worm #12-22, Trico #22, Walt's Worm #8-16.

All of these flies can be tied unweighted or weighted with wire or beads.

Nelson Haines

Small dry flies for Spring Creek: top to bottom, left to right. Cream Midge, Female Trico spinner, Griffith's Gnat, Blue-winged Olive Sparkle Dun, Black Midge, Tiny Blue-winged Olive.

Wet Flies

Light Cahill #12-14, Orange Cahill #12-14, Soft Hackles (Tan, Gray, Olive, Yellow, Orange) #12-18, Sparkle Caddis Pupa #14-18, Sulfur #12-18, Wet Ant #12-18.

Streamers

Shenk Minnow #4-10, Shenk Sculpin (black, white) #4-10, Woolly Bugger (black, white chartreuse, tan, brown, olive/black) #4-12.

Dry Flies

Ant #10-24, Beetle #10-20, BWO #18-24, Cranefly #16-18, Caddis (tan, tan/olive, grayish tan/dark olive, grayish tan/cream) #14-18, Cahill (orange, yellow) #10-16, Cricket #12-16, Flying Ant #16-28, Griffith's Gnat #20-24, Midge (black, white, olive, gray, ginger, brown) #18-28, Sulfur #12-18, Trico #22-24.

Attractor dries such as Humpies and Patriots are also worth trying.

Tributaries

"...a poisonous substance is said to have overflowed into the stream from the Central Pennsylvania Gas Company's plant at Axemann. Scenes reminiscent of fish hauls made by Coleville residents several weeks before when hydrated lime found its way into Buffalo Run were re-enacted by persons living along Logan Branch north of the gas plant. Trout from five to over 20 inches long were gathered up by the tub and basket full." *Pennsylvania Angler*, July, 1939 The maximum fine for polluting streams was only $100.00 at that time.

Spring Creek's tributaries used to be top quality trout streams in their own right, overshadowed because of the world-class fishery they fed. The feeders have suffered from different types of pollution and/or water depletion. Nonetheless, opportunities still exist on a few streams.

Cedar Run and Mackey Run are limestone feeders that join at Linden Hall and meet Spring Creek at Oak Hall. Formerly open to the public, they were posted because of poor behavior of some anglers.

Roaring Run, Galbraith Gap Run (also known as Jack's Mill Run), and the upper end of Slab Cabin Run all drain Tussey Ridge. They have remnant populations of the watershed's original brook trout. Most of Galbraith Gap Run is posted.

Slab Cabin Run offers some fishing — when it flows. Trout migrate into the stream from Spring Creek. This stream joins with Thompson Run in Millbrook Marsh, a short distance from Spring Creek in Houserville. Thompson Run flows all year and maintains a year-round trout fishery. Because of siltation, however, holding water is scant.

Gap Run flows off Nittany Mountain into Pleasant Gap, where it sinks. Like the Tussey Mountain feeders, it has a small brook trout population that has somehow managed to survive logging, road building and runoff, water diversion and illegal dumping. Its sister stream, McBride Gap Run (also known as Rockview Gap Run) is posted by Rockview Penitentiary.

Buffalo Run is a small, brushy limestone stream. It used to offer fantastic fishing and was so dependable that, during my fish-killing days, I went there when I wanted trout to eat. It is no longer as good. Development and attendant dewatering and siltation have taken their toll, and the average size of trout is down -- when the stream flows.

Logan Branch is the largest and best known of Spring Creek's tributaries. It has an excellent trout population, but is not as easy to fish as Spring Creek. Pools are short and small, rendering good evening fishing frustrating. Holes and riffles are likewise short and often overhung, and a recurring problem faced by anglers there is spooked trout. A true spring creek, Logan Branch's food chain is limited in diversity. The stream makes up for that with the quantity of what it has — sowbugs, shrimp, and sulfurs. The trout fare so well on the bountiful subsurface feed that the stream is notorious as a poor dry fly destination. Axemann resident Tim Bixler lamented the poor dry fly fishing behind his house. "I have never seen so many flies come off of a similar sized piece of water. But I have only seen two trout rise there all season!" Consistently successful anglers on the stream are locals who have fished it all their lives and know how and when to tackle each spot. There are many posted properties along Logan Branch, as well as some of the meanest dogs that I have encountered while fishing!

One thing anglers should beware of when fishing the smaller tributaries is the presence of rattlesnakes. Most of the small streams are close to if not "in" the mountains surrounding the watershed. Snake sightings are common. Most of the rattlers that I have seen have been on mountain streams and roads in the area. If you do not like snakes, let alone enjoy fishing in very tight brush, leave the little streams alone.

Conservation

Spring Creek's fishery would not be what it is today without the efforts of local conservationists. The Spring Creek Chapter of Trout Unlimited (SCTU) was founded in 1973, and was the stream's only advocate group for years. The organization remains the most consistent and combative voice for Spring Creek. SCTU has had its share of defeats, but also some stellar victories. Most notable have been the Chapter's roles in the Nease Chemical pollution, designating Spring Creek as a high quality coldwater fishery, rerouting Thompson's Spring, and the imposition of catch and release management. Without these achievements, Spring Creek's fishery would not be worth the effort of this book. Chapter members can be proud of their record.

The Spring Creek Watershed Community provides a full forum for discussion of the variety of activities going on in the watershed. Conservation as well as non-conservation organizations and interested individuals make the Community a venue for anglers and the non-angling public who would like to support the preservation of Spring Creek. General goals include enhancement of the watershed's environment and quality of life. Hopefully, successes by this organization will benefit Spring Creek. The Watershed Community is closely tied to the ClearWater Conservancy.

The ClearWater Conservancy was formed in 1980 to protect land and water resources in Centre County. Its mission statement includes preservation of open spaces and natural habitats, conservation of water, and creation of a watershed based approach to land use and development. Under ClearWater's charter as a land trust organization, the Conservancy has secured preservation of some watershed land through purchases and easements. The Conservancy has a full time office and staff.

The Spring Creek Watershed Commission was

Willy and Betsy Shields enjoying trout fishing at Spring Creek Park.
Future generations will not know the joy of fishing if we do not protect our resources.

created in 1996 to coordinate watershed projects by local municipalities. The Commission has been active in creating stormwater management plans and in applying for state grants to further community goals such as a Spring Creek greenway. The Commission is composed of the Centre County Commissioners and representatives appointed by the 14 municipalities in the drainage basin.

These organizations are necessary to Spring Creek's survival and restoration. The fishery is still great, even if impaired. Imagine what it could be if it were improved beyond its current productivity!

Priority Projects for Conserving Spring Creek

Minimum flows should be established for watershed streams. Hydrologists can determine groundwater levels necessary to maintain streams at trout-friendly temperatures. When groundwater approaches base levels, water use restrictions should be implemented starting with questionable uses such as lawn watering and graduating to other functions.

No water should be permitted to be drawn directly from watershed streams.

Areas critical to the recharge of aquifers should be identified and conserved. Much of Spring Creek's groundwater comes from small drainages on flanking ridges. These rills must be protected and allowed to flow unimpeded into their respective sinkholes. A

moratorium on pond building on these small watersheds is needed to conserve groundwater recharge. Existing ponds that impound natural flows should be removed.

Undeveloped land should be conserved for water table recharge. Penn State University and Rockview Penitentiary are good places to start. Their unused land should be turned into parkland or green space. Any attempt to develop this land should be countered. State forest land in the watershed should be expanded to further help this process. Conservation easements for water table recharge and riparian protection should be encouraged.

A goal of 100% sewage recycling in the drainage should be set. Recycle plans should include discharge in a way that recharges groundwater.

Improve stormwater detention basins. They should trap, filter, and permit water to seep into the ground instead of pollute streams. Big offenders include the Bryce Jordan Center, I-99 and University Park Airport basins. But the Duckpond (including its feeder ditch) is the worst. Water runs so quickly through the Duckpond that it fails to trap silt and contaminants efficiently, and there is a five-plus degree surge in temperature in Thompson Run after big summer storms. Such discharge is not permitted to individuals and businesses. Why is it legitimate for State College and Penn State? All springwater currently diverted into the Duckpond should be routed around

45

it. "The Duckpond's discharge is bad for Spring Creek. Spring Creek needs good water desperately, and here is a supply we're not using intelligently. Here is a priority project for Trout Unlimited and ClearWater Conservancy. Any efforts to defend the current way water is run through the Duckpond should be regarded as supporting continued pollution of Spring Creek." Joe Humphreys

Permeable pavements and parking lot designs that permit water to drain into the ground instead of running off have been refined. Future building codes in the drainage should incorporate permeable pavement.

Establish riparian buffers for all streams and sinkholes in the drainage. Buffers should be a minimum of 20 feet wide. Government managed land, including Fish & Boat Commission properties, should serve as showcases. Stream bank stabilization and channel narrowing (where necessary) should be included as part of good riparian buffers. Anglers notice that there is better habitat where banks are not eroded. The channels are deeper and less silty than wide, shallow reaches.

Develop methods for containment and disposal of silt and gravel runoff from roadside ditches. I-99 and the Benner Pike are the biggest runoff contributors. Smaller roads, however, often contribute a greater amount of sediments in proportion to their size. Prime examples exist in Lemont, where Mount Nittany Road, Thompson Street, and the alley behind the Post Office run off large amounts of silt and gravel into Spring Creek.

Insist that quarries discharging water into local streams adhere to thermal and wastewater guidelines for coldwater streams. A great place to start would be the quarry that pipes water to the Pleasant Gap hatchery.

Purchase more properties along the stream for public access. Interested parties can set up a fund to do so. Those people who enjoy the stream will be there to defend it.

These are not the only problems facing Spring Creek, just the ones most important today. Fish & Boat Commission hatchery discharges would have made this list, but the Commission is actively planning upgrades that should diminish the ill effects of their effluent. The fishery can also be enhanced by habitat improvements and preserved by catch and release regulations. Such efforts will be to naught, however, if Spring Creek dries up.

Spring Creek now relies almost entirely on man's beneficence. It is a paradox that a stream whose productivity was a result of the Creator's gifts now relies on man's conservation efforts to keep it alive. If you read this book in the distant future, please visit Spring Creek. Ask if it flows, and if it is still a wild trout fishery. If not, find out who killed it. Please hold

those responsible to public account. Many people have worked hard to protect and improve Spring Creek. It's your turn.

Watershed Services

These businesses offer something of interest to local and visiting anglers. They all have some inherent quality of location, function, or service.

Fly Shops/Fly Tackle
Outdoor Wear/Camping/Ski/Paddlesports

Flyfisher's Paradise
2603 East College Ave., State College, PA 16801
Phone: 814-234-4189 FAX: 814-238-3686
www.flyfishersparadise.com   Very popular website!
M-Th 12-6, Fri. 12-8, Sat. 10-5 Closed Sunday
Flyfisher's Paradise is one of the east's premier fly shops. Richardson Chest Fly Boxes, Orvis, Sage, Cortland, Loomis, Ross, Scientific Anglers, Mustad, Stearns, Regal, Renzetti, Umpqua, Metz, Books, Fly tying, Flies, Gift Certificates, Catalog.

The Richardson Chest Fly Box® Co.
860 Pleasant View Blvd., Suite 1, Bellefonte, PA 16823
Phone/FAX 814-353-3188
www.chestflybox.com
email: chesflybox@aol.com
The original chest fly box, first made in 1951 and now known around the world. These hand built metal boxes last a lifetime and can be customized to the angler's specs. These are the best (unqualified) chest boxes available.

Appalachian Ski and Outdoors
123 South Allen St., State College, PA 16801
Phone: 814-234-3000 or 800-690-5220
http:\\www.theadventuresource.com
email: outdoors@the adventuresource.com
This is the place in State College for quality clothing and equipment for camping, backpacking, travel, climbing, mountaineering, downhill and cross-country skiing, snowboarding and paddlesports. Major name brands like Patagonia, North Face, Columbia, Kelty, Ex Officio, Rossignol and others are stocked. The knowledgeable staff uses the products and can explain how to get the best performance from them.

Flyfishing Instruction/Classes

Mark Antolosky and Daniel Shields
Flyfisher's Paradise, Phone: 814-234-4189
www.flyfishersparadise.com
We have enjoyed teaching almost three thousand students in the last twenty years. We provide individual and group lessons for beginning and advanced anglers,

Casting and nymph Fishing Classes, FFF Certified Casting Instruction. See www.flyfishersparadise.com for a list and description of classes.

Vance McCullough

2114 North Oak Ln., State College, PA 16803
814-237-9683
www.statecollege.com/mcc/flyfish
Vance succeeded his mentor, Joe Humphreys, as "Penn State's Fly Fishing Professor." He has fished trout streams across North America and uses his extensive teaching experience to relate stream tactics and techniques into targeted lessons for beginners as well as more advanced anglers. Sessions can include teaching with a guided trip.

Guide Service (Insured)

GDP Adventures

62 South Parsons Drive, Mill Hall, PA 17751
570-893-6474
email: grandeck@cub.kcnet.org
GDP guides work Spring, Penn's, Fishing and Spruce Creeks and the Little Juniata River. They have full and half day rates, and offer stream orientation trips in addition to standard guiding. These fellows have a good history of satisfied clients. GDP guides do not fish while you are left unattended.

Bed & Breakfast

Accommodations B&B

200 Houserville Rd., State College, PA 16801
Phone: 814-238-5195
Accomodations is less than 100 feet from Spring Creek upstream from Spring Creek Park in Houserville. I have spent many pleasant hours fishing this water. This is the closest of the B&Bs listed in this book to Penn State and downtown State College. Accommodations has two, fully appointed, private guest rooms.

Reynolds Mansion

101 West Linn St.,Bellefonte, PA 16823
814-353-8407 or 800-899-3929
reynoldsmansion.com
email: innkeeper@reynoldsmansion.com
This Victorian landmark has to be seen to be believed. Reynolds Mansion is located among many wonderful old houses that lend a great ambiance to the neighborhood. The owner fly fishes and can provide helpful information and directions.

Spring Creek House B&B

1088 West Water St., Bellefonte, PA 16823
Phone: 814-353-1369
www.springcreekhouse.com
email: Mikegruendler@hotmail.com
This B&B has 250 feet of Spring Creek frontage between Fisherman's Paradise and Bellefonte. Fish Commission surveys consistently rate the water in front of the B&B as some of the best in Pennsylvania. The building itself has an interesting history.

Camping

Both campgrounds are located close to Exit 161 of I-80, and are well located for fishing Spring, Fishing, and Bald Eagle Creeks. Both campgrounds are clean and well run by the owners, who told me that they do not tolerate rowdy guests. I have never heard any complaints about either campground. Cabins, too! **Camping is not permitted on Fish & Boat Commission property.**

Bellefonte KOA

2481 Jacksonville Rd.,Bellefonte, PA 16823
Phone: 814-355-7912
koa.com

Fort Bellefonte Campground

Rt. 26, 2023 Jacksonville Rd., Bellefonte, PA 16823
Phone: 814-355-9820, 800-487-9067

Cottages

Eagle Rock Cottage

205 Yorkshire Ln, Bellefonte, PA 16823
814-355-2694
www.eaglerockcottage@nb.net
This fully equipped cottage can accommodate up to six guests. Eagle Rock is located a few yards from Spring Creek downstream from Fisherman's Paradise. There is excellent fishing right in front of the cottage! This is a popular place for many anglers.

Photographic Equipment, Film Developing

The Camera Shop

311 West Beaver Ave., State College, PA 16801
Phone: 814-237-5326
This place is incredibly helpful. They have patiently answered my neophite photographic questions without making me feel like an idiot. The Camera Shop also does a good job digitizing photos.

Dining

The Gamble Mill Tavern

160 Dunlop St., Bellefonte, PA 16823

Phone: 814-355-7764

www.gamblemill.com

Fine dining for lunch and dinner in a casual atmosphere. This 200-year old mill is built over a millrace diverted from Spring Creek. There is good fishing right beside the Gamble Mill's parking lot. Nobody ever complains about getting invited to eat here!

Sheetz Convenience Stores

2814 East College Ave., State College, PA 16801

Phone: 814-231-8133

765 Benner Pike, State College, PA 16801

Phone: 814-861-6400

Sheetz are the best area convenience stores. The Benner Pike location is handy to Benner Spring and Fisherman's Paradise. It is at the junction of Route 150 and Shiloh Road. The College Ave. store is right across the street from the upper end of Spring Creek. You can get a variety of subs made to order (my favorites) and other goodies. Both stores also have ATM's, pay phones, gas, and air.

Motels

The Autoport Motel and Restaurant

1405 South Atherton St., Bus. Rt. 322

State College, PA 16801

Phone: 800-932-7678 or 814-237-7666

http://autoport.statecollege.com

My mother likes this place. It is well maintained and clean. It is centrally located to fish area waters, and you do not have to drive through downtown State College to do so. Good food makes this a local favorite for fast breakfast, pleasant lunch, moderate and upscale dinners. Excellent Sunday brunch. Pool.

The Bush House and Schnitzel's Tavern

315 High St., Bellefonte, PA 16823

Phone: 814-355-4230

The Bush House is an historic old style hotel in downtown Bellefonte that has accommodated anglers for over a century! Schnitzel's Tavern is located in the hotel, and is a great place to eat. It has an outdoor patio beside Spring Creek where you can watch the trout while you dine!

Colony Lodge Motel

3482 Benner Pike, Bellefonte, PA 16823

Phone: 814-355-5561 or 800-500-4656

www.colonylodge.com

This motel the closest one (about a mile) from Fisherman's Paradise. It is also the closest motel to Benner Spring. It is moderately priced and well located to get around the area without having to drive into downtown State College.

Resorts

Toftrees Resort and Four Star Golf Club

One Country Club Ln., State College, PA 16803

Phone: 800-252-3551, 814-234-8000

www.toftrees.com

The only resort between Harrisburg and Pittsburgh also happens to be located a few miles from Spring Creek! This is a full service resort with an 18-hole, four star golf course, two restaurants, a 100-room hotel, and a conference center. Check their website or call for information about packages.

Retreats

Harvest Fields Ministry Center, Inc.

1100 East Boal Ave., PO Box 77, Boalsburg, PA 16827

Phone: 814-466-9201

info@harvestfields.com

This is a lovely property on the outskirts of Boalsburg. It is a beautiful venue for meetings, weddings, retreats, etc. Guests can obtain access to private bass ponds on site. There is one overnight guest suite. No alcohol permitted.

Afterword

Readers of my earlier book, *Penn's Creek River Journal,* will notice the difference in tone between that book and this one. *Penn's Creek River Journal* was easier to write because of a less urgent conservation mission. It is hard to write about Spring Creek in anything but a concerned tone because of the sad history of the stream. The ravages of pollution are a default underlay to the fishery.

Anglers fishing Spring Creek always have the potential for disaster in the back of our minds. We must do what we can to heal the hurts that this marvelous stream has suffered and head off future tragedy.

Other books written or compiled by Daniel Shields

Penn's Creek River Journal, by Daniel Shields

George Harvey: Memories, Patterns and Tactics narrated by George Harvey, compiled by Daniel Shields

Both available through your local fly shop, or contact: DLS Enterprises, PO Box 41, Lemont, PA 16851